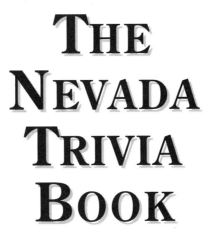

THE NEVADA TRIVIA BOOK

Third Revised Edition

By Richard Moreno

Gem Guides Book Co.
315 Cloverleaf Drive, Suite F
Baldwin Park, CA 91706

Dedicated to Pam, Hank and Julia,
the three most important people in my life.

And to Dad and Mom,
for being not only good parents, but great people.

4

CONTENTS

INTRODUCTION 5
BOOMTOWNS AND BUSTS 7
Events and People in Nevada History
GAMBLING AND ENTERTAINMENT...............48
Casino Capital of the World
MINING LORE...74
Untold Wealth Lost and Found
GEOGRAPHY 95
Places and the People Who Made Them
THE FIRST NEVADANS 121
Indian Culture and Myth
COWBOYS AND COWTOWNS. 135
From Ranches to Rodeos
NATURAL NEVADA.......................................145
Landscape of Grandeur
SCOUNDRELS AND STATESMEN 166
Politics in the Silver State
FASCINATING FACTS....................................186
Vital Statistics of the Sagebrush State
QUICK FACTS ABOUT NEVADA....................204
BIBLIOGRAPHY 206
INDEX 212
ABOUT THE AUTHOR 237

Introduction

◊◊◊◊◊◊◊◊◊◊◊◊◊◊◊◊◊◊◊◊◊◊◊◊◊◊◊

Nevada may be the most misunderstood of states. To some, it is neon-drenched hotel-casinos, acres of green felt tables, gallons of free cocktails and such glamorous, mostly single-named entertainers as Cher, Sammy, Barbra and Celine. To others, the place conjures up images from the past: rickety, worn-down ghost towns, leather-skinned cowboys roaming the wide open range in search of lost cattle and wide spots in the road where the waitress at a local diner still calls everyone "Hon."

The truth is that Nevada is all of those things—and more. It defies easy description because it is so diverse. And that's part of what I love about Nevada. It's still possible in this slightly eccentric, mostly unpretentious, largely uncluttered state to know your governor by first name, drive on the wrong side of a lonely stretch of country road when you feel the urge because you don't see anyone for twenty-five miles in either direction or order a chicken fried steak without feeling guilty.

Nevadans who live out in the hinterlands—the state is more than 110,000 square miles in size—are a hearty breed. In some places they must drive more than an hour to get to a grocery store or gas station, a couple of hours to reach a hospital and most of a day to get to a city big enough to have a department store.

And Nevada's cities aren't like everyone else's. Sure, there are the usual trappings—endless miles of subdivisions, traffic jams, fast-food joints and occasional bad air—but only in the Silver State can you visit a pyramid, meet the Cowardly Lion, hang out with dolphins and play slot machines in the supermarket.

Nevada has a way of grabbing your imagination. Maybe that's because of its infatuation with the fantastic, best manifested in the state's otherworldly hotels and shows. Or, perhaps, it is the rich, colorful tales about this still-young raw state that make it so fascinating.

This is a book about some of those facts and stories. It's about people like James "Old Virginny" Finney, who supposedly broke a bottle of whiskey on the main street of a new mining camp—then used the occasion to christen the community, Virginia City, in honor of his birth state—as well as Sarah Winnemucca Hopkins, one of the first Native Americans to pen a book about the plight of her people.

Although there's nothing trivial about Nevada's history, places and people, these wonderful facts and figures are presented in a question and answer format to make them fun to read.

Maybe you'll discover something you may not have known and decide to learn a little more about Nevada. Special thanks to Phil Earl, former curator of history at the Nevada Historical Society, Ron James of the Nevada Division of Historic Preservation, the Las Vegas News Bureau, Rich Johnston of the Nevada Department of Transportation, David Moore of *Nevada* magazine, Rick Dower, Martin Griffith, Dennis Myers and Nevada State Archivist Guy Louis Rocha, a tireless champion of historical accuracy and an invaluable resource.

I hope you enjoy.

Richard Moreno

BOOMTOWNS AND BUSTS

❖❖❖❖❖❖❖❖❖❖❖❖❖❖❖❖❖❖❖❖❖❖❖❖

Q: What was the name of the first organized wagon train party to cross Nevada on its way to California?

A: In 1841, the Bidwell-Bartleson Party became the first wagon train to travel across Nevada to California. Led by John Bidwell and John Bartleson the group traveled from the Great Salt Lake, across the salt flats, then along the Humboldt River, before crossing the Sierra at Sonora Pass.

Q: What country owned the territory that included Nevada in 1843?

A: The Republic of Mexico controlled much of today's American West, including Nevada.

Q: Who was the first non-Indian on record to have set foot in the region that would become Nevada?

A: The first non-Indian to cross into Nevada was Father Francisco Garcés a Spanish explorer who was seeking a more direct route between Santa Fe and Monterey. In the spring of 1776, Garcés and two Indian guides crossed the southern tip of Nevada.

Q: In the 1850s, what two territories, which later became states, originally included the land that became the state of Nevada?

A: The northern three-quarters of Nevada was part of the Utah Territory, while the southern quarter was part of the New Mexico Territory (and later became part of the Arizona Territory).

Q: What Nevada county was once part of Arizona?

A: Clark County in southern Nevada was part of the Arizona Territory until 1867.

Q: When was the Nevada Territory created?

A: The Nevada Territory was established by Congress on March 2, 1861 and was signed by President James Buchanan the same day.

Q: Where did the first train robbery in the western U.S. take place?

A: The first train robbery in the West occurred on November 4, 1870 at Laughlin Springs, east of Reno. The crime was planned and perpetrated by "Smiling Jack" Davis, a Virginia City stable manager.

Q: Whose divorce in 1906 focused worldwide attention on Reno and Nevada's "quickie" divorce laws?

A: In the Corey Divorce, Laura Corey traveled to Reno to take advantage of the state's short residency requirements. She won a $2-million divorce settlement from her husband, William Corey, who was president of the U.S. Steel Corporation.

Q: In 1936, what southern Nevada city was almost as large as Las Vegas?

A: Boulder City, a planned community built by the federal government to house workers on the Hoover Dam project had nearly as many residents (about 6,000) in the late 1930s.

Q: True or false, the portrait of Abraham Lincoln, painted by Charles M. Shean which hangs in the Nevada State Assembly chambers, was the model for the Lincoln face engraved on the $5 dollar bill?

A: False. This is a common misconception probably created because the U.S. Government considered three different portraits for the engraving, including the Shean painting, which was not used. Today, Shean's Lincoln is on display at the Nevada Historical Society in Reno.

Q: What was the name of the tragic emigrant wagon train group that became trapped in the Sierra Nevada Range during the severe winter of 1846 to 1847?

A: The ill-fated group was the Donner Party, whose members attempted to cross the Sierra, near present day Donner Lake, in October 1846. They became stranded in heavy snow for months. By the time relief parties reached them, forty-four of the eighty-seven members of the party had perished.

Q: What famed mountain man, working for the Rocky Mountain Fur Company, became the first white man on record to cross the center of Nevada?

A: Jedediah Smith, who traveled through southern Nevada in 1826, became the first white explorer to cross central Nevada when he led a small party from the Sierra Nevada Range, which he crossed at Ebbetts Pass, to the south shore of the Great Salt Lake in Utah. The journey consumed about five months and roughly followed the path of modern day Highway 6 through Nevada.

Q: Where and when did Nevada's first recorded marriage take place?

A: According to Thompson and West's 1881 *History of Nevada*, the first wedding is believed to have occurred at Gold Canyon near present-day Dayton) in 1853. A man named Powell arrived in the area with his motherless family, which included his daughter, fourteen-year-old Mary. While Powell was away on business, a miner named Benjamin Cole convinced Mary to marry him. The two were wed by a visiting justice of the peace. Cole left his bride with Mrs. Walter Cosser while he went off to build a cabin. Powell returned, discovered his daughter had married without his permission, and wanted to take her to California along with the rest of his family. Local residents were divided in their sympathies and conflict seemed inevitable. To avoid bloodshed, Powell and Cole agreed to let Mary decide whether to go with her father or remain as Cole's wife. She chose to go with her father and the marriage was dissolved—thereby making it the state's first marriage and divorce.

John C. Fremont
Photo courtesy of Nevada Historical Society

Q: Who was the first white man on record to see Lake Tahoe?

A: Famed explorer John C. Fremont spotted the lake in 1844 while traveling through the mountains to the south. Fremont traveled across Nevada during explorations of the region in 1843 to 1845. His report to the U.S. Congress, which included the first accurate maps of the region, helped open the previously unknown area.

Q: Who was the first non-Indian woman to cross Nevada?

A: Nancy Kelsey, who traveled across the Great Basin region in 1841 as a member of the Bidwell-Bartleson Party.

Q: What former World Heavyweight Boxing Champion once worked in mining camps and saloons in Tonopah?

A: Jack Dempsey the "Manassas Mauler", bounced around the Tonopah area doing a number of jobs in the early 1900s. In 1919, he defeated Jess Willard to become the Heavyweight Champion of the World.

Q: What famed boxing promoter, who built the original Madison Square Gardens in New York, once owned a saloon in Goldfield?

A: G. L. "Tex" Rickard owned and operated the Northern Saloon in Goldfield from about 1905 to 1908. In September 1906, Rickard promoted a world middle-weight boxing championship match in Goldfield between Joe Gans and Oscar "Battling" Nelson. The fight garnered international publicity and established Rickard's national reputation as a boxing promoter.

Famed boxing promoter G.L. "Tex" Rickard originally owned this brick Victorian house, which is still standing in Goldfield.

Q: What explorer discovered the Humboldt River, following it from its source to its sink?

A: In September 1828, trapper and explorer Peter Skene Ogden crossed into Nevada near the present town of Denio. He traveled south and encountered the Humboldt River on November 9, 1828. The next year, he returned and followed the river to its ending point at the Humboldt Sink, near present-day Lovelock.

Q: What survivor of the "Shootout at the O.K. Corral" later became a deputy sheriff in Goldfield?

A: Virgil Earp, brother of lawman Wyatt Earp, moved to Goldfield in 1904. Shortly after arriving, he was hired as deputy sheriff of Esmeralda County and worked as a security officer for the National Club. In the fall of 1905, Virgil Earp contracted pneumonia and died in Goldfield on October 19, 1905. He was buried in Portland, Oregon.

Q: What famous former Tombstone, Arizona, lawman operated a saloon in Tonopah in 1902?

A: Famed gunman Wyatt Earp and his wife, Josie, lived in Tonopah for seven months in 1902. During his brief time there, he worked as a Deputy U.S. Marshal and as a teamster, and was part owner of the Northern Saloon.

Q: Who was the first non-Indian to die in Nevada?

A: Joseph Paul, who died in 1828. Paul was a trapper with Peter Skene Ogden's party that traveled through northern Nevada that year.

Q: Who led the first group of tourists to Nevada?

A: Actress Lola Montez and a small party departed from Grass Valley, California, for an excursion to the Truckee Meadows, in July 1853, becoming the first tourists ever to visit the state.

The Northern Saloon
Photo courtesy of Nevada Historical Society

Q: What event in California created a massive influx of people to the state, most of whom crossed Nevada?

A: The famous California Gold Rush was sparked by the discovery of gold at Sutter's Mill, near Coloma, California, on January 24, 1848. Within a year, nearly 25,000 people flocked to California, most traveling through Nevada.

Q: What year was Nevada's first seal approved?

A: The first territorial seal was approved during the First Regular Session of the Legislative Assembly of the Territory of Nevada on November 29, 1861. The seal was described as: 'Mountains, with a stream of water coursing down their sides, and falling on the over-shot wheel of a quartz mill at their base; a miner leaning on his pick, and upholding a United States flag, with a motto expressing the two ideas of loyalty to the Union and the wealth to sustain it, Volens et Potens ("Willing and Able").'

Q: What popular Virginia City prostitute was murdered in 1867 and said to have been given one of the largest and most elaborate funerals the city had ever seen?

A: Julia Bulette was a legendary courtesan who was said to be so well-liked she was named an honorary member of Virginia Fire Engine Co. 1. On July 2, 1867, a laundry worker, John Millian, was convicted of robbing and murdering Bulette. He was hanged on April 23, 1868, with some 4,000 people—including writer Mark Twain—looking on.

Q: When was the first formal government organized in Nevada?

A: On November 12, 1851, a public meeting was held at the Mormon Station in Genoa to establish laws and a governing body for western Nevada. The group agreed to elect a governing council with seven members and established a system for making land claims. A second meeting was held on November 19, which declared timber lands common property, and a third was held on November 20, during which those present elected a justice of the peace, clerk and sheriff. The government, which was never recognized by the U.S. government, ceased to exist in 1855, with the arrival of officials from the Utah Territory.

Genoa

Q: Where was the first courthouse in Nevada?

A: A small wooden courthouse was constructed in Genoa, county seat of Carson County in the Utah Territory, in 1860.

Q: What was the first permanent settlement established in Nevada?

A: The first permanent settlement is generally believed to be Genoa, which was established in June 1851 as a trading post by John Reese. The post, originally referred to as Mormon Station, was also the first lasting structure built in Nevada. However, there has been disagreement about Genoa's claim to be Nevada's first settlement because of evidence that several miners, including James Finney, had been living in Gold Canyon, near the present day site of the town of Dayton, beginning in 1850. Historians and others continue to debate whether the miners' presence in Gold Canyon constitutes a permanent settlement.

Q: When was the State of Deseret, which included most of present-day Nevada and Utah, crafted by Brigham Young and the Mormon Church?

A: On March 18, 1849, the Church of Jesus Christ of Latter Day Saints (Mormon Church) organized the State of Deseret and elected church leader Brigham Young as governor. The action was not recognized by the U.S. Congress and the petition for statehood was rejected.

Q: When was the Reno area first settled?

A: In 1852, H. H. Jameson, established a trading post for travelers on the Emigrant Trail in the Truckee Meadows.

Q: When was the Carson City area settled?

A: In November 1851, Frank and Joseph Barnard, George Follensbee, Frank and W. L. Hall and A. J. Rollins opened a trading post at what today is the intersection of Thompson and Fifth Streets in Carson City. The post was named Eagle Station.

Q: When did the first transcontinental overland mail route cross Nevada?

A: Initial service of the "Jackass Mail" (so-called because letters were carried by mules) started from Sacramento on May 1, 1851, crossing into Nevada a few days later. The mail service was offered once a month.

Q: Where and when was the first post office established in Nevada?

A: The first post office in the state was established at Carson in Utah Territory in December 1852. In 1854, the Carson post office name was changed to Genoa.

Q: What was the dreaded Forty-Mile Desert?

A: This name was given to the approximately forty-mile stretch of sand and sagebrush that separated the Humboldt Sink, which was the end of the Humboldt River, and the Carson River. This dry, inhospitable part of the Emigrant Trail, which claimed many lives, was considered to be the most difficult part of the entire journey.

Q: In 1852, who claimed jurisdiction over the area that includes the present state of Nevada?

A: On March 3, 1852, the Utah Territorial Government (created by Congress on September 9, 1850) passed a measure extending the boundaries of seven of its counties into the area that is now

Nevada. In 1855, Utah Territory officials appointed judges and political representatives for the area, which was named Carson County. Utah Territory's political control continued until 1857, when Mormons living in the area were called back to Salt Lake City during tensions between the Mormon Church and the U.S. government. Carson County government was reestablished in 1859.

Q: What was the name of the trading post that offered the first water and supplies for emigrants who survived the Forty-Mile Desert?

A: This oasis, established about 1850 on the banks of the Carson River (near present-day Fallon), was called Ragtown because many emigrants, upon arriving, often washed their dust-caked clothing in the river and hung them in the trees to dry.

Q: When was the right to vote for political candidates in Nevada extended to nonwhite males?

A: This change was made in 1880, yet still excluded Indians.

Q: Who was the first African-American settler on record in Nevada?

A: Benjamin Palmer settled in the Carson Valley, near Sheridan, in 1853. He operated a ranch there for forty years.

Q: When was the first stagecoach crossing of the Sierra Nevada Range into Nevada?

A: The first stagecoach to navigate the Sierras was in June 1857, when a coach traveled from Placerville, California to Genoa, Nevada. Regular stagecoach service was started shortly after.

Mormon Fort, Las Vegas

Q: What was the first white settlement established in southern Nevada?

A: A Mormon mission was started in June 1855 in the Las Vegas Valley. The mission was abandoned within two years.

Q: When was the first permanent settlement established in the Las Vegas area?

A: In 1865, Octavius Decatur Gass took ownership of the Old Mormon Fort, which had been abandoned in 1858, and established a station to supply the Las Vegas Valley and travelers to California. He named his settlement "Los Vegas Rancho."

Q: What was the Mormon War, and what was its impact on the area that would become Nevada?

A: The so-called Mormon War (or Utah War) was the result of long-standing disagreements and mistrust between officials of the Mormon Church in Utah and the U.S. government. In 1857, President James Buchanan appointed new officials for the Utah Territory and sent a military force to aid in the enforcement of federal laws, primarily those banning polygamy. Mormon Church leader Brigham Young, who considered the action an invasion, issued a call for all Mormons to return to Salt Lake City to defend the community in the event of a war. By late September 1857, most Mormons in Nevada had abandoned their farms and homes, which were eagerly acquired by non-Mormons.

Q: What year did the bicycle arrive in Nevada?

A: Two-wheel bicycles were introduced to the state in 1869.

Q: Who was the first non-Indian believed to have visited the Las Vegas Valley?

A: Rafael Rivera, a young Mexican scout with a trading party that was traveling on the Spanish Trail (located about 100 miles south of Las Vegas), is believed to have ventured north to the Las Vegas Springs in about 1829.

Q: In the 1870s, what Virginia City hotel boasted the first hydraulic elevator in Nevada?

A: This pioneering elevator was in the elegant International Hotel, which was six stories high.

Q: Approximately how many people lived in Nevada when it became a state in 1864?

A: Only an estimated 40,000 people resided in the newly created state of Nevada.

Q: When was Reno incorporated?

A: Reno was first incorporated as a city in 1897 and disincorporated in 1899. The State Legislature incorporated the city again in 1903.

Q: Where did the first balloon ride occur in Nevada?

A: In July 1868 Tony Ward lifted off in a hot air balloon from Carson City.

Q: What was Nevada's first commercial television station?

A: Television KLAS in Las Vegas began broadcasting on July 22, 1953.

Q: What was Nevada's first commercial radio station?

A: Radio station KOH (now known as KKOH) in Reno began officially broadcasting on November 1, 1928. Nevada's first licensed radio station was KDZK, which began broadcasting from the Majestic Theater in Reno in 1922. The station, owned by the Brioli Family, was non-commercial and initially broadcast for one hour a night.

Q: What was the state's first newspaper?

A: The *Gold-Canon Switch*, a small, handwritten sheet produced in 1854 in the mining camp of Johnstown, near present-day Virginia City, was Nevada's first newspaper.

Q: What was the first newspaper to be regularly published in Nevada?

A: The venerable *Territorial Enterprise* was the state's first regular paper, appearing for the first time on December 18, 1858, in Genoa. A year later, it was moved to Carson City, then, in 1860, to Virginia City, where it achieved its greatest fame.

Q: Where was Nevada's first daily newspaper published?

A: *The Silver Age*, the state's first daily, began publishing in Carson City as a weekly paper in 1860. On August 26, 1861, the paper converted to daily frequency and became the first daily in Nevada. On November 2, 1862, the paper was moved to Virginia City, where it became the *Virginia Daily Union*.

Q: When did the first Chinese settle in Nevada?

A: Chinese people from San Francisco went into the Carson Valley in 1855 to help construct irrigation ditches. By 1870 there were 3,150 Chinese living in Nevada, which represented about six percent of the state's total population.

Q: What explorer first surveyed the Central Overland Wagon Road Route through Nevada for the U.S. Army?

A: Captain James H. Simpson of the U.S. Army surveyed the road in May-June of 1859. It shortened the California Trail by almost 300 miles and roughly parallels present-day Highway 50.

Q: What was the first settlement in the Truckee Meadows (later Reno)?

A: In 1859 C. W. Fuller built a small hotel and crude toll bridge near a ford on the Truckee River for travelers going from Honey Lake, California to Virginia City. In 1861, he sold the property to Myron C. Lake, who, in 1868, negotiated with the Central Pacific Railroad to develop the town site that became Reno.

Q: For whom is Reno named?

A: Reno was named by Charles Crocker, superintendent of the Central Pacific Railroad and his partners, in honor of General Jesse Lee Reno, a Union officer killed during the Civil War at the Battle of South Mountain, Maryland, in 1862.

Q: When did the first telegraph line reach Nevada?

A: The first telegraph line was constructed between Placerville, California, and Genoa in late 1858. It was extended to Carson City in 1859 and to Virginia City a year later. Called the Placerville & Humboldt Telegraph Company Line, it was part of the first transcontinental telegraph system.

Q: What famed British explorer traveled over the Pony Express route in 1860 ?

A: Sir Richard Burton, discoverer of Lake Tanganyika and the first white man on record to enter the Moslem holy city of Mecca, traveled via the Pony Express route in September and October of 1860. He maintained a detailed diary, which provides one of the best eyewitness accounts of the route.

Q: How long did the Pony Express operate through Nevada?

A: This famed express mail service, which carried letters by horseback between St. Joseph, Missouri, and Sacramento, California, operated in Nevada for a total of eighteen months, from April 1860 to October 1861.

Q: When was Nevada's first "bank holiday" called by state regulators?

A: On November 1, 1932, state officials called the first of many "bank holidays" due to the failure of several banks in the state owned by financier George Wingfield. These holidays were designed to prevent depositors from making a run on a particular bank that was in precarious financial condition and allowed regulators time to reorganize failing institutions.

Q: What was Nevada's first bank?

A: In 1860, the Wells Fargo Express and Banking Company opened an office in Virginia City, which was the state's first bank.

Q: What event in the early 1860s was variously described as the Roop County War, the War of Injunctions and the Sagebrush War?

A: The so-called war was a dispute that erupted in 1863 between California and the Nevada Territory over the boundary line between the states. The matter was finally resolved when both agreed to a joint boundary survey, which was accepted by the California legislature on April 4, 1864, and the Nevada legislature on February 7, 1865.

Remains of Sand Springs Pony Express Station near Sand Mountain, located fifteen miles east of Fallon.

Q: What year was alfalfa introduced in Nevada?

A: Two Washoe County ranchers, Peleg Brown and Irvin Crane, first planted alfalfa in Nevada in 1862. The crop became the state's most widely planted and important agricultural product.

Q: What other names were considered by the Territorial Constitutional delegates before the name Nevada was decided upon for the thirty-sixth state?

A: The state was actually called Washoe in a legislative draft of 1862. Other names discussed by the delegates included Humboldt and Esmeralda.

Q: What is the only community designated as one of the original county seats by the territorial legislature of 1861 that has kept that distinction without any changes?

A: Virginia City, which has been the seat of Storey County since 1861. As an aside, Carson City was the original seat of Ormsby County, but its status changed when the city and county were consolidated into a single municipal government in 1969.

Q: What Nevada city was the first in the state to boast gas lights?

A: Booming Virginia City holds that distinction. In 1862, a gas plant and lights were installed in the Queen of Comstock in booming Virginia City. Reno didn't have a gas light system until 1876.

Q: Over the years, how many railroads have operated in Nevada?

A: Approximately sixty individual major and minor railroads have operated in Nevada. Many were short lines that extended only a few miles.

Q: When was the Nevada State Prison established?

A: The Nevada State Prison was established in 1862 in the Warm Springs Hotel, located east of Carson City. The state leased the land for two years, then purchased it in 1864. The building

The Nevada State Museum, constructed between 1866 and 1869, was originally the Carson City Mint.

burned in 1867 and a new prison, still standing, was constructed the following year. The prison's first warden was Abraham Curry, founder of Carson City.

Q: When was the famed Carson City Mint built?

A: The mint, which coined silver from nearby Virginia City, was constructed between 1866 and 1869. Construction took three years because the U.S. government failed to pay for the project in a timely manner. The mint was used until 1895 and the machinery dismantled in 1899. In 1939, it was sold to the State of Nevada and was restored as the Nevada State Museum.

Q: What was the result of the first election to approve a state constitution for Nevada, held on January 19, 1864?

A: The measure failed by a wide margin—8,851 votes to 2,157—because it called for mines to be taxed at the same rate as other property, which was opposed by the mining industry. A second constitution was drafted in July 1864, which exempted mines and mining claims from being taxed like other property, and was approved by voters on September 7, 1864 by a margin of 10,375 to 1,284.

Q: Where does Virginia City get its water?

A: In 1873, the Virginia City and Gold Hill Water Company constructed an ingenious system of pipes and flumes to transport water from Marlette Lake, high above Lake Tahoe, to the two Comstock communities. The system includes twenty-one miles of pipe and forty-five miles of flumes, and is still in use. In 1975 it was designated a national landmark by the American Society of Civil Engineers.

Q: What was the original name of the town of Yerington?

A: This sleepy agricultural community was originally called Pizen Switch, a name derived from the local whiskey, which was called "poison" or "pizen." The "switch" referred to the fact that the local saloon was made of willows and was called Willow Switch. Later, the town was, for a short time, called Greenfield.

Q: What Nevada town was said to have been named in honor of a railroad official, in the hope he would be enticed to locate his line through the community?

A: The town of Yerington, seat of Lyon County, was named after Henry M. Yerington, superintendent of the Virginia & Truckee and Carson & Colorado Railroads. According to legend, the townspeople chose the name in the hope that Yerington would

**The town of Yerington, which for many years proclaimed
itself "Cattle Kingdom in the Copper Hills," was
originally named "Pizen Switch."**

extend the C&C line through their community, but he located
the line twelve miles north in Wabuska. The tale, however, isn't
true since the town was named after Yerington in 1894, which
was more than a decade after the railroad had been built
through Wabuska.

Q: When did the first railroad engine enter Nevada?

A: On December 13, 1867 the first locomotive from the Central
Pacific Railroad edged across the state line near present-day
Verdi. Construction of the line, which started in Sacramento,
California, had begun on January 8, 1863, and took five years
because of difficulties in building over and through the Sierra
Nevada Range.

Q: What was the name of the rail line that once connected eastern California to the Virginia & Truckee Railroad line?

A: The Carson & Colorado, started by a consortium that included many of the principals in the V&T, was built between 1880 and 1883 to connect the Owens Valley area of California (and the mines of Bodie and Candelaria) with the transcontinental railroad at Reno via the V&T line at Mound House, Nevada. Originally narrow gauge, the line was purchased by the Southern Pacific Railroad in 1900 and converted to standard gauge. The portion of the line between Mound House and Fort Churchill was abandoned in 1934, followed by abandonment of the stretch between Mina and Benton in 1938. The line ceased operating in 1960.

Q: Where was the first all girls private school in Nevada?

A: Bishop Whitaker's School for Girls was opened on October 12, 1876 in Reno. Run by the Episcopal Church, the school operated until 1894.

Q: Who established the first private school in Nevada?

A: Hannah K. Clapp and Ellen Cutler established the Sierra Seminary in Carson City in 1862. The school was the first private, co-educational facility in the state. In 1877, Clapp, Eliza Babcock, and Annie Martin started the first kindergarten class in the state, also in Carson City. In 1887, at the age of sixty-three, Clapp became the first female faculty member at the University of Nevada, which had relocated that year to Reno from Elko.

An interesting historical footnote: In August 1875, she and Eliza Babcock were the successful bidders to construct an iron fence around the new State Capital, which had been completed in 1871. The two businesswomen made a $1,000 profit.

Hannah K. Clapp
Photo courtesy of Nevada Historical Society

Metropolis

Q: What early twentieth-century agricultural development floundered after Lovelock farmers successfully sued to restrict water?

A: Metropolis was an ambitious development that sought to build a city of 7,500 people in 1909. Promoters envisioned 40,000 acres of cultivated crops fed by a dam on the Humboldt River. Unfortunately, although lots were sold and the dam, a hotel and school were built, the developers neglected to secure water rights. In 1913, down-river farmers from Lovelock successfully sued to prevent the diversion of the river behind the dam and the town was doomed. By the late 1940s, the town was abandoned.

Q: When did Las Vegas get its first post office?

A: On August 1, 1855, when a post office was established at the Mormon colony (also called the Mormon Fort) that had been founded earlier that year. The post office was named Bringhurst, after William Bringhurst, one of the colony's leaders.

Q: Before the Washoe County seat was moved to Reno in 1871, where was it?

A: Washoe County's first seat of government was located in Washoe City, a small town south of Reno in Washoe Valley. By the early 1870s, Reno had began to thrive as a regional transportation hub, and was able to wrest the seat from its smaller neighbor.

Q: Where was the first telephone system in Nevada installed?

A: In 1877, electric telephones were installed in Virginia City's mines. These small, private systems were the first phone networks in the state.

Q: Where and when was the state's first municipal telephone service established?

A: Frank Bell cousin of Alexander Graham Bell helped install Nevada's first city phone service in Reno in 1886. Bell was also Nevada's lieutenant governor from 1889 to 1890, and, following the death of Governor C. C. Stevenson in late 1890, served as acting governor for four months. In 1894, the Sunset Telephone & Telegraph Company wired all of Reno for phone service, becoming the first municipal telephone system in the state. The first long distance telephone service became available in Reno in 1899.

Q: Where were the first electric street lamps installed in Nevada?

A: The Reno Electric Light Company installed the first electric street lights on February 4, 1887. Electric street lights came to Carson City a year later.

**This massive crater on the Nevada Test Site depicts
the incredible energy released during an above ground
atomic bomb test conducted in the 1950s.**
Photo courtesy of the Nevada Historical Society.

Q: When was the Nevada Proving Ground (later called the Nevada Test Site) opened?

A: The Nevada Proving Ground was established by the U.S. Atomic Energy Commission in southern Nevada in December 1950 to test nuclear weapons. Above-ground atomic testing began in 1951 and continued until 1962, when it was shifted underground. Originally 680 square miles, the test site was expanded to 1,350 square miles—an area slightly larger than Rhode Island—in the mid-1950s.

Q: Under what nom de plume did Virginia City journalist William Wright write?

A: Wright was better known by his pseudonym Dan De Quille in the pages of the legendary *Territorial Enterprise* newspaper.

Q: What unusual phenomenon in the Pahranagat Valley did nineteenth century western writer Dan De Quille make famous?

A: De Quille wrote a mock serious article about the famous rolling rocks of Pahranagat. According to De Quille, the earth's magnetic field would cause huge boulders to roll down to the valley floor, then, depending on the time of day, to roll back up the valley's sides. The article attracted national attention—showman P. T. Barnum offered to pay to have the rocks perform in his circus—before De Quille admitted it was a hoax.

Q: What year was the first public library established in Nevada?

A: In 1895 the Nevada legislature authorized the state's first public library in Reno.

Q: What was the first municipal streetcar system in Nevada?

A: The Reno Traction Company built a fixed rail streetcar system in Reno in 1904. The line operated until 1927, when it was replaced by buses.

Q: When was Nevada's first highway designated?

A: Nevada Route 1, which stretched across the northern part of the state from Wendover to Verdi, was designated in 1913. Later, it was named the Victory Highway (1920), then U.S. Highway 40 (1926) and finally, Interstate Highway 80 (1958).

Q: When was the first transcontinental crossing of the United States by automobile, which included a trip across northern Nevada?

A: From May 23 to August 1, 1903, a caravan of autos traveled across the country to demonstrate the practicality of long distance auto travel. The cars crossed Nevada using roads that are part of today's Interstate Highway 80, reaching Winnemucca on June 21 and Elko on June 23.

Q: What was the first movie theater in Nevada?

A: The Vitagraph Theater in Reno opened in 1903 and was the state's first movie house.

Q: Where did the world's first execution by lethal gas take place?

A: Nevada holds the macabre distinction of being the first place in the world to carry out an execution using lethal gas. The condemned was a convicted murderer named Gee Jon, who was executed at the Nevada State Prison in Carson City in 1924.

Q: What was the nation's first federal water reclamation project?

A: The Newlands Reclamation Project, also called the Truckee-Carson Project, was authorized by the U.S. Congress in 1902. Named in honor of the U.S. Senator Francis G. Newlands of Nevada, the project was grand in scope, involving the construction of 104 miles of canals, 504 miles of laterals and 335 miles of open ditches–all designed to move water from the Truckee and Carson Rivers to a dry spot in the desert that would be transformed into an oasis.

Q: What famous boxing match, held in Carson City on March 17, 1897, was the first legal prize fight in the United States?

A: The Jim Corbett-Bob Fitzsimmons fight, held on a site at what today is the corner of Musser and Harbin Streets, was Nevada's first world championship fight, the first legal prize fight in the country and the first filmed prizefight. Fitzsimmons beat the champion, "Gentleman Jim" Corbett in the fourteenth round.

Q: What famous heavyweight boxing match was held in Reno on July 4, 1910?

A: World Heavyweight Boxing Champion Jack Johnson defended his title against former champion Jim Jeffries in Reno on that date. The match gained worldwide notoriety because Johnson was an African-American and Jeffries was billed as the "Great White Hope." Johnson won the bout.

Lahontan Dam, constructed in 1914, is part of the Newlands Water Project, the first federal reclamation project.

Q: When was Clark County created?

A: Clark County, which features Las Vegas as its seat, was approved by the Nevada legislature on July 1, 1909.

Q: Who was the only woman to ever be legally hanged in Nevada?

A: In June 1890, Elizabeth Potts was sent to the gallows, along with her husband Josiah, for the murder of Miles Faucett.

Q: When was the city of Las Vegas established?

A: Las Vegas was founded as a stop on the San Pedro, Los Angeles and Salt Lake Railroad on May 15, 1905. The city was formally incorporated in 1911.

Nevada Governor's Mansion

Q: When was the Nevada Governor's Mansion built?

A: The southern colonial mansion, located in Carson City, was built during 1908 to 1909. The home was designed by Reno architect George Ferris and Company and cost $22,700. The first governor to live in the mansion was Denver S. Dickerson.

Q: Where did the last stagecoach robbery in the western U.S. take place?

A: The West's last stagecoach robbery occurred on December 5, 1916 at Jarbidge Canyon in northern Elko County.

Q: When did construction begin on Hoover Dam?

A: Work on this massive public works project started in 1931 and continued until March 1935. The dam was officially dedicated in September 1935.

Q: Where did the first air flight in Nevada take place?

A: A Curtis biplane climbed fifty feet and traveled a distance of about a half-mile in a field about three miles north of Carson City on June 23, 1910. It was the first air flight in the state and the first ever from such a high altitude (4,675 feet).

Q: Where did the first Trans-Sierra airplane flight land?

A: Three DeHavilands and a Curtis trainer landed in a field three miles east of Carson City (today, it would be in front of Carson High School) on March 22, 1919. The flyers, who started at Mather Field in Sacramento, were welcomed by Governor Emmet Boyle, who flew with them on their return flight—making him the first civilian to cross the Sierra in flight.

Q: Where was the first airmail service in Nevada?

A: On April 6, 1926, Varney (later called United) Air Lines inaugurated the first regularly scheduled trans-continental airmail service. The first airmail flight in Nevada landed in Elko.

Q: Where was Nevada's first dude ranch built to take advantage of the state's liberal divorce laws?

A: The first dude ranch was at Sutcliffe on Pyramid Lake, north of Reno. It was built in 1929 following passage of a bill by the Nevada legislature that reduced the residency requirement for divorce from six to three months. The dude ranch business boomed after 1931, when the legislature reduced the requirement to six weeks.

The Lehman Caves in the Great Basin National Park contain fascinating stone formations.

Q: In what year was the Lehman Caves National Monument created by the U.S. Congress?

A: Congress established Nevada's first national monument in 1922. The monument encompassed about 5,000 acres in eastern Nevada, including Lehman Caves, a series of underground passages filled with unique limestone formations. In 1986, the Lehman Caves National Monument became part of the Great Basin National Park.

Q: What Nevada writer penned *The Ox-Bow Incident* and *Track of the Cat*?

A: Walter Van Tilburg Clark (1909–1971) gained fame as the quintessential western writer with those two books, both made into movies. He was born in Maine, but moved to Reno at the age of eight. He attended local schools and graduated from the University of Nevada, Reno (UNR). His father, Dr. Walter E. Clark, served as university president from 1917 to 1938. Nevada was a frequent setting for his stories.

Q: What western artist-writer wrote his best-known work, *Smoky*, while living in Washoe Valley?

A: Will James (1892–1942) lived on a small ranch in Washoe Valley during the mid-1920s. In 1924, he wrote *Smoky*, a tender story about a wild mustang that became a classic western novel.

Q: What is Nevada's oldest continuously published magazine?

A: *Nevada* magazine, originally called *Nevada Parks and Highways*, has been published by the state of Nevada since 1936. The name was changed in 1975.

Q: What University of Nevada, Reno (UNR) graduate was the basis for the main character of Ernest Hemingway's *For Whom the Bell Tolls*?

A: Robert Hale Merriman (1909–1938) graduated from UNR in 1932. In 1937, he joined the Abraham Lincoln Brigade, a military battalion consisting of idealistic Americans who had joined in fighting against the forces of General Francisco Franco in the Spanish Civil War. Within a short time he became commander and befriended Hemingway, a war correspondent. Later, Hemingway incorporated elements of Merriman's life and personality in the character, Robert Jordan, who appeared in *For Whom the Bell Tolls*.

Q: What year was the University of Nevada founded?

A: Although the state's constitution, approved in 1864, called for the establishment of a university, a school wasn't actually opened until 1874.

Q: Where was the first University of Nevada located?

A: From 1874 to 1886, the university operated in the small northeastern Nevada community of Elko. In 1886, it was moved to Reno, where it is today.

Q: When was the University of Nevada, Las Vegas started?

A: The University of Nevada began offering extension classes in Las Vegas in 1951 (originally held at Las Vegas High School). Three years later, the Nevada Southern University branch was established as a permanent part of the university system and, in 1957, opened its first building, Maude Frazier Hall, on a sixty-acre site on Maryland Parkway in Las Vegas. The school began issuing degrees in 1963 and became the University of Nevada, Las Vegas in 1969.

Q: What was the first building on the University of Nevada, Reno campus?

A: Morrill Hall, still standing, was the first structure, built in 1887. It was named for U.S. Senator Justin S. Morrill of Vermont, author of the Morrill Land Grant Act of 1862, which led to the establishment of the University of Nevada system.

Q: What Nevada-born writer has written several books about Basques and Basque-Americans?

A: Robert Laxalt, born in Carson City in 1923, is author of several important books about Basques, including *Sweet Promised Land, A Cup of Tea in Pamplona, Basque Hotel* and *Child of the Holy Ghost.*

Morrill Hall, erected in 1885, is the oldest building on the campus of the University of Nevada, Reno.

Q: Where is the annual National Basque Festival?

A: Elko in northeastern Nevada has a large Basque-American population and hosts this celebration.

Q: When did Basques begin to arrive in Nevada in large numbers?

A: In 1870, Basque rancher Pedro Altube began running sheep and cattle in Elko County. Soon, he was bringing other Basques from Europe to work on his ranch, paying them in livestock. Usually, the sheepherder could acquire his own band of animals and start his own outfit. A number of sheep ranches in Nevada, Oregon and Idaho started this way.

Basque dancers perform a traditional dance at the annual National Basque Festival in Elko.
Photo by C.J. Hadley

Q: What is the oldest Basque hotel in Nevada?

A: The Winnemucca Hotel is the oldest of the dozen or more Basque hotels in Nevada. It was constructed in 1863 as a Basque hotel and continues to serve Basque family-style meals.

Q: What did Mormon elder Orson Hyde do to the citizens of Genoa in 1862?

A: Hyde placed a curse on the citizens. He was angry because non-Mormon Genoans took Mormon holdings without payment after the Mormons were called to Salt Lake City by church leader Brigham Young during a dispute between the church and the U.S. government.

Q: In the 1930s, what did women seeking "the cure" in Reno traditionally do after receiving their divorce decree?

A: According to popular legend, these newly freed women would kiss the pillar in front of the Washoe County Courthouse, then toss their wedding rings into the nearby Truckee River. Pioneering Reno advertising executive Thomas C. Wilson, however, later revealed that Reno Chamber of Commerce folks frequently smeared lipstick on the courthouse columns and tossed cheap dime store rings into the river to encourage the myth.

Q: By what name was the Lovelock area called by pioneers on the Emigrant Trail?

A: This fertile valley was called Big Meadows because of the availability of grass and water. Many wagon trains regained their strength and collected new provisions at Big Meadows before embarking across the dreaded Forty-Mile Desert, which was the next part of the journey to California.

Q: Why was the town of Minden created?

A: Minden was founded in 1906 after rancher H. F. Dangberg offered the Virginia & Truckee Railroad a right-of-way through his land in return for a terminus of the tracks. The name honors Dangberg's birthplace in Germany.

Q: What was the first hotel built in Nevada?

A: The Rogers & Thorington House, built at Genoa in 1857, was the first hotel constructed in the state. The two-story hotel provided lodging for stagecoach passengers and for travelers on the Emigrant Trail.

Q: What is the oldest continuously operating hotel in Nevada?

A: The Gold Hill Hotel, near Virginia City, has been operating since 1859.

Q: What was Nevada's first resort?

A: Walley's Hot Springs, built in 1862, near Genoa, was the first resort hotel in the state. The complex included a two-story hotel with hot mineral springs.

Q: What notorious Comstock bad man was shot in self-defense by pioneer Carson Valley rancher Henry Van Sickle?

A: Sam Brown, who allegedly killed eleven men and robbed countless others, sought to kill Van Sickle, who had apparently loaned his pistol to a member of a posse that had hunted Brown a year earlier. On July 6, 1861, Brown stopped at Van Sickle's Station to settle his grudge. Van Sickle, however, got the drop on the outlaw and killed him with his shotgun.

Q: What was the name given to Las Vegas' notorious red-light district, which operated openly from about 1905 to 1941?

A: Las Vegas' sex district was called "Block 16," reflecting its designation on the city plats. The district was finally closed during World War II, when the War Department threatened to declare the entire city of Las Vegas, including its casinos, off-limits to servicemen unless the area was shut down.

Q: What famed nineteenth-century newspaper editor barely survived a stagecoach ride with famed driver Hank Monk over the Sierra Nevada Range?

A: The editor was Horace Greeley (of "Go west, young man" fame), who, in 1859, hitched a ride with the legendary Monk, a driver on the Overland Mail Stage Route. Greeley wanted to get from Carson City to Placerville as quickly as possible. Monk raced over the mountains, bouncing Greeley with such violence that he allegedly lost the buttons off his coat. The humorous tale of the journey was told by Mark Twain in *Roughing It*.

Q: During the Pyramid Lake Indian War, what legendary Pony Express rider once rode 380 miles, stopping only to eat, change horses and take brief rests?

A: "Pony" Bob Haslam was forced to make this ride in May 1861. He set out from Friday's Station, at Lake Tahoe, for Buckland's Station, east of present-day Dayton. Upon his arrival, however, the next scheduled rider refused to take the mail because of the hostilities with the Paiutes. Haslam agreed to continue (for a $50 bonus) and rode all the way to Smith Creek. After a nine-hour rest, Haslam attempted to return but found the next station at Cold Springs had been attacked and burned by Indians. He rode almost straight back to Friday's Station—completing the 380-mile loop in record time.

Q: How much beer was sold to the 20,000 residents of the booming mining town of Virginia City in 1880?

A: A staggering 225,000 gallons of beer was sold that year—or about fifteen gallons per person.

Q: By what name was pioneer skier Jon Torsteinson Rui known?

A: Rui, who introduced skiing to the West, was better known as John "Snowshoe" Thompson. Born in Norway, Thompson arrived in California in 1854 and two years later began carrying mail between Placerville and Genoa. He delivered mail for nearly two decades and died in 1876. He is buried in Genoa.

Q: The daughter of which Comstock Silver King married Herman Oelrichs, a member of one of the most prominent families in New York high society?

A: She was Tessie Fair, daughter of James Graham Fair, who was one of the richest mining owners on the Comstock. Tessie Fair married Herman Oelrichs, a member of a prominent shipping family. In 1902, Tessie Fair and her sister, Virginia, began construction of San Francisco's famed Fairmont Hotel as a monument to their father.

Glendale School

Q: What is the oldest school building in Nevada?

A: The Glendale School, built in 1864, originally was located on the eastern side of the Truckee Meadows (part of modern-day Sparks). The building was used until 1958; then, in 1993 it was moved to downtown Sparks to become part of the Heritage Park and Museum.

Q: What famous American songwriter/composer was married to the granddaughter of Comstock Silver King John Mackay?

A: The composer was Irving Berlin (1888–1989), who was married for 62 years to Ellin Mackay, granddaughter of John W. Mackay.

Q: Where in Nevada were the first "Levi" jeans invented?

A: The first pair of "Levis" were sewn in 1870 by a Reno tailor named Jacob W. Davis. The pants were made for a gigantic-size woodcutter—he had a fifty-six-inch waist!—who kept bursting out of his other clothing. Davis used a durable, white cotton canvas called No. 7 Duck, and added rivets to hold the pocket corners and seams. Davis' invention was an immediate success. To meet the demand, in 1872, he became partners with Levi Strauss, a San Francisco materials supplier. Noticing that white cloth was difficult to keep clean, Strauss changed the material to a blue, woven cotton twill from France called "serge de Nimes," which was later shortened to "denim."

GAMBLING AND ENTERTAINMENT
Casino Capital of the World
❖❖❖❖❖❖❖❖❖❖❖❖❖❖❖❖❖❖❖❖❖

Q: What was the largest slot machine jackpot ever won in Nevada?

A: The largest slot machine jackpot in Nevada history was $39.7 million, won at the Excalibur Hotel-Casino in Las Vegas on March 21, 2003.

Q: What was the name of the Las Vegas hotel-casino built by gangster Benjamin "Bugsy" Siegel?

A: The Flamingo was the name of the luxurious hotel-casino constructed under the direction of Bugsy Siegel. Opened on December 26, 1946, the $5-million property was the first full-service resort built in Nevada after World War II and the third built on The Strip. Siegel, who spent more than double the original estimate on building the hotel, was suspected by his gangland partners of siphoning money for himself and was murdered in Beverly Hills in June 1947.

Q: Does Nevada have a state lottery?

A: Surprisingly, no. State law prohibits lotteries in Nevada.

Q: What western-themed 1940s hotel-casino, the second opened on the Las Vegas Strip, once picked up visitors at the airport with a horse-drawn stagecoach?

A: The Last Frontier, which opened on October 30, 1942, used an authentic stagecoach to take patrons from the airport to the hotel. In 1955, the property was expanded, renovated and renamed the New Frontier. It was revamped again in 1967 and became simply the Frontier.

Q: Who coined the name, "The Strip," for Las Vegas Boulevard, which was also called the Los Angeles Highway?

A: Former Los Angeles Police Captain Guy McAfee who purchased the Pair-O-Dice Club on the Los Angeles Highway in 1938 and reopened it as the 91 Club, is credited with calling Las Vegas Boulevard, "The Strip." He said the road reminded him of L.A.'s Sunset Strip between Hollywood and Beverly Hills.

Q: What was the first hotel-casino in Nevada to offer big-name entertainment as an incentive to attract customers?

A: Surprisingly, it wasn't in Reno or Las Vegas where name entertainment first arrived in Nevada. In 1941, the Commercial Hotel in Elko booked Ted Lewis and his orchestra for an eight-day engagement at a cost of $12,000. The resulting publicity attracted record crowds and owner Newton Crumley followed with other performers, such as Paul Whiteman, Tommy and Jimmy Dorsey and the Andrews Sisters. Elko's initial competitive advantage quickly evaporated when clubs in Reno and Las Vegas followed suit.

Q: What was the first gambling corporation in Nevada to become a publicly traded company?

A: Harrah's in September 1971.

Q: What was the name of the first legal gambling casino licensed in the state of Nevada?

A: The first was the Northern Club on Fremont Street in downtown Las Vegas, which received Clark County gaming permit No. 1 on March 20, 1931. In Northern Nevada, the first legal casino was the Owl Club at 142 Commercial Row in Reno, which was granted a permit on March 26, 1931.

Photo courtesy of Nevada Historical Society

Q: When was gambling legalized in Nevada?

A: On March 19, 1931, Governor Fred B. Balzar, here shown between Death Valley Scotty (left) and Will Rogers, signed an act legalizing gambling in Nevada. The act took effect immediately.

Q: What other scandalous legislation was approved by the Nevada legislature and signed by the governor on the same day?

A: Governor Balzar also signed a bill lowering the residency requirement for a divorce in Nevada to six weeks. The act took effect on May 1, 1931.

Q: What Reno casino made a worldwide name for itself with its innovative advertising slogan that ended with the words, "...Or Bust?"

A: Harolds Club, which beginning in the 1940s placed billboards proclaiming "Harolds Club or Bust," throughout the U.S. and in selected locales around the world, including the North Pole. At one point, the casino had 2,300 billboards carrying its slogan. Most, however, were dismantled in 1965 following passage of the Federal Highway Beautification Act.

Q: What was Las Vegas' first nightclub with legal gambling?

A: The Meadows was the city's first true nightclub. Opened in 1931, it was located on the road between Las Vegas and Boulder City (to attract men working on Hoover Dam), and boasted the first floor shows in the state.

Q: When did Nevada start a state tax on gaming revenues?

A: In 1945, the Nevada legislature passed a law shifting authority to grant gambling licenses from local and county officials to the state tax commission. At the same time, the legislature approved a tax of one percent of gross earnings. The tax was increased to two percent in 1948, then to a progressive scale of three and a half to five and a half percent, depending on amount of revenues in 1955. Today, it is six and one-fourth percent of earnings.

Q: What was the first major resort built on the Las Vegas Strip?

A: On April 3, 1941, the western-themed El Rancho Vegas opened on The Strip with sixty-three rooms, a two hundred fifty-seat dining and showroom, and casino.

Q: Who was the first big-name entertainer to appear in a Las Vegas resort?

A: In January 1944, Sophie Tucker appeared for two weeks at the Last Frontier. Her appearance kicked off a period of intense competition for name entertainment at hotels throughout the state.

Q: What was the first high-rise hotel-casino built in Las Vegas?

A: The Apache, which opened on Second and Fremont Streets in 1932, was called the first high-rise in the city, standing three stories, with one hundred rooms. It boasted the first elevators in Las Vegas. The first modern high-rise was the nine-story Riviera Hotel on the Las Vegas Strip, constructed in 1955.

Q: What was the first skyscraper built in Nevada?

A: In 1947, the twelve-story art deco Mapes Hotel-Casino opened in Reno. The towering hotel was the tallest building in the state until 1956 when the fifteen-story Fremont Hotel was opened in downtown Las Vegas.

Q: What was the world famous slogan of Reno's Harolds Club Casino?

A: The words, "Harolds Club Or Bust," affixed to a covered wagon became famous during the 1940s, 1950s and 1960s as a result of an advertising campaign. The signs appeared throughout the country on billboards, the tops of barns, and on a sign at the North Pole. The club even asked NASA to place a Harolds Club sign on the moon during the first lunar landing in 1969. Harolds Club was started in 1936 by Raymond I. "Pappy" Smith and his two sons, Raymond A. and Harold.

At 1,149 feet, the Stratosphere Tower in Las Vegas is the tallest building in the state of Nevada.

Photo Courtesy of the Nevada Commission on Tourism.

Q: What is the tallest building in Nevada?

A: The Stratosphere Tower in Las Vegas is 1,149-feet high, which makes it the tallest building west of the Mississippi and the tallest free-standing observation tower in the United States. It weighs more than 100 million pounds and contains 290 miles of rebar, which is approximately the distance between Los Angeles and San Francisco. It has the world's highest roller coaster, which runs around the outer edge of the tower's crown, and the world's highest thrill ride, the Space Shot, which catapults riders upward on a vertical track at the top of the tower.

Q: What is the tallest building in Northern Nevada?

A: The Silver Legacy Hotel tower, which is 37 floors or more than 400-feet high.

Q: What airline started regularly scheduled service between Reno and Las Vegas in 1945?

A: Bonanza Airlines, which later became part of Hughes Air West, started the first regular service between the state's two major metropolitan areas.

Q: What is the name of the giant neon cowboy figure that has been a fixture at the Pioneer Club in downtown Las Vegas since 1947?

A: "Vegas Vic" is the moniker of the friendly neon cowboy who towers above Glitter Gulch.

Q: Where is "Glitter Gulch" in downtown Las Vegas?

A: Fremont Street, now known as the "Fremont Street Experience" for its five-block long, ninety-foot overhead canopy displaying spectacular neon light shows.

Q: What was the first paved street in Las Vegas?

A: Fremont Street in downtown Las Vegas became the city's first paved boulevard in 1925.

Q: What U.S. president performed on stage at the Last Frontier in Las Vegas?

A: Former President Ronald Reagan, an actor in the thirties and forties, made his only stage appearance in the state (not counting his years in office) in 1954.

Q: When and where did Frank Sinatra first perform in Las Vegas?

A: The future "Chairman of the Board" first appeared on a Las Vegas stage in 1951 at the Desert Inn.

"Fremont Street Experience"
Photo courtesy of Las Vegas News Bureau

Q: What Las Vegas hotel-casino gained fame in the 1960s as a favorite hangout of the "Rat Pack," a group of entertainers that included Frank Sinatra, Dean Martin, Sammy Davis Jr., Joey Bishop and Peter Lawford?

A: The Sands Hotel-Casino was the meeting place for these legendary gatherings.

Q: What casino introduced female blackjack dealers?

A: In the early 1940s, Harolds Club in Reno, followed quickly by Harrah's Club, introduced women dealers. Prior to World War II, dealers were male in most casinos. Labor shortages during the war years spurred clubs to hire women.

Q: What is the largest hotel in Reno?

A: The Reno Hilton is the largest with 2,003 rooms.

Wayne Newton

Q: What was the name given to the city of Reno's ordinance that for many years restricted gambling?

A: The regulation, drafted in 1947, was frequently called the "Red Line Ordinance" because a red line was actually drawn around a commercial district along Virginia Street downtown. Gaming was not allowed outside the area. The ordinance stayed in effect until 1970.

Q: What euphemism is used to describe gambling in most Nevada promotional literature?

A: The apparently less offensive term, "gaming," is frequently used by Nevada politicians and in tourism promotional materials to describe the state's number one industry.

Q: What singer opened the showrooms of both the International Hotel (now the Las Vegas Hilton) in 1969 and the MGM Grand Hotel and Theme Park in 1993?

A: Barbra Streisand was the opening entertainment for both properties, which were, not coincidentally, owned by Kirk Kerkorian.

Q: What famed telethon has been held in Las Vegas every Labor Day weekend (except in 1990) since 1973?

A: The Jerry Lewis Muscular Dystrophy Telethon has been held at various hotels and other venues, including the Sahara Hotel-Casino and Caesar's Palace, since 1973. The exception was the twenty-fifth anniversary show in 1990, which was held in Los Angeles.

Q: What popular Las Vegas performer is called the "Midnight Idol?"

A: Wayne Newton, who has played in Las Vegas hotels since 1959 (he dropped out of high school to play at the Fremont), is called the "Midnight Idol" as well as the "King of Las Vegas." In 1996, he celebrated his 25,000th Las Vegas performance.

Q: What popular British rock n' roll quartet performed two concerts at the Las Vegas Convention Center in 1964?

A: The Beatles made their only Las Vegas appearance in August 1964. The group played to capacity crowds of 8,500 at each show.

Q: What community was originally to be called Casino, Nevada, but was denied by the U.S. Postal Service?

A: Laughlin, Nevada, was originally proposed to be "Casino" by Don Laughlin, the town's founder and owner of the Riverside Hotel-Casino in Laughlin. Postal authorities suggested using his name after turning down "Casino."

Q: What is the largest casino in Nevada?

A: The MGM Grand Hotel in Las Vegas has the biggest casino with gambling space covering 171,500 square feet.

Q: What performer, frequently identified with Las Vegas, made a less than impressive debut at the New Frontier in 1956 and didn't perform there again for thirteen years?

A: Elvis Presley made an unsuccessful appearance in Las Vegas in 1956, despite already having several hit songs. His rock n' roll music apparently did not find many fans among the New Frontier's audience of older gamblers. In 1969, however, he made a triumphant return to Las Vegas with sold-out shows at the International (now the Las Vegas Hilton).

Q: What famous eccentric purchased the Castaways, Desert Inn, Frontier, Landmark, Sands and Silver Slipper Hotels in Las Vegas and Harolds Club in Reno, between 1966 and 1970?

A: Reclusive industrialist Howard Hughes purchased all of those properties during that four-year spending spree. His empire was broken up following his death in 1976.

Q: How many tourists visit Nevada each year?

A: According to the Nevada Commission on Tourism, 48.6 million visitors traveled to Nevada in 2003, with about 36.7 million visiting Las Vegas.

Q: How much revenue do Nevada casinos bring in?

A: According to the Nevada Gaming Control Board, gamblers left more than $9.6 billion in Nevada casinos in 2003.

Q: Are horse racing and dog racing legal in Nevada?

A: Both are legal, although there haven't been any tracks offering those sports on a regularly scheduled basis since the mid-1970s.

**Elvis lives again in the Legends in Concert show
at the Imperial Palace, Las Vegas.**

Showgirls in the Folies Bergere circa 1987
Photo by Las Vegas News Bureau

Q: What Las Vegas casino offers an opportunity to have your photograph taken standing next to $1 million in cash?

A: Every day, between 4 p.m. and midnight, Binion's Horseshoe Club in downtown Las Vegas offers a free photo taken in front of one hundred $10,000 bills.

Q: What hotel was the first to introduce topless showgirls in a Paris-style revue?

A: The Dunes Hotel was the first to offer a show with bare-chested dancers with its presentation of *Minsky Goes to Paris*, in 1957.

Q: What is the longest running production show in Las Vegas history?

A: The longest running revue is the Folies Bergere at the Tropicana Hotel and Casino, which began in 1959 and is still drawing crowds.

Q: What was the first revue show in Nevada to feature rows of leggy, dancing, sequined showgirls?

A: The show was *Lido de Paris*, a revue imported from Paris, which opened in July 1958 at the Stardust Hotel in Las Vegas and ran until 1991.

Q: What percentage of the state of Nevada's general fund revenues are derived from taxes on gambling?

A: Approximately forty-five percent of the state budget relies on gambling taxes.

Q: What percentage of Nevada's work force is directly employed by the gambling industry?

A: One-third of all jobs in Nevada are directly related to the gambling industry.

Q: When did Nevada allow public corporations to own gambling properties?

A: In 1967, the Nevada legislature approved a bill allowing a public corporation to own a casino without requiring the licensing of every shareholder. The change in law allowed corporations to invest in the gaming industry, dramatically increasing financial resources available for the development of new hotels and expansion of existing properties.

Mirage Hotel-Casino
Photo courtesy of Mirage Hotel-Casino

Q: True or False, Las Vegas is home of eight of the 10 largest hotels in the world?

A: True. The world's ten largest hotels are:
1. Ambassador City Jomtien, Thailand – 5,100 rooms
2. MGM Grand Hotel & Casino, Las Vegas – 5,005 rooms
3. Luxor, Las Vegas – 4,408 rooms
4. Mandalay Bay (including Hotel), Las Vegas – 4,341 rooms
5. Venetian, Las Vegas – 4,049 rooms
6. Excalibur, Las Vegas – 4,008 rooms
7. Bellagio, Las Vegas - 3,993 rooms
8. Circus Circus, Las Vegas – 3,774 rooms
9. Flamingo Las Vegas – 3,565 rooms
10. Hilton Hawaiian Village, Hawaii – 3,386 rooms

Q: What Las Vegas hotel-casino boasts an artificial volcano and dolphin pond?

A: The Mirage Hotel-Casino on the Las Vegas Strip, which also displays rare white tigers, has a volcano attraction that erupts every half hour.

Q: Which of the following can you legally bet on in Nevada?
  A) State elections
  B) Presidential elections
  C) The University of Las Vegas Running Rebels basketball team
  D) All of the above

A: C is the correct answer.

Q: What Nevada community ranks third in gaming revenues, after Las Vegas and Reno?

A: Laughlin ranks third after Las Vegas and Reno.

Q: What is Nevada's "Black Book?"

A: The "Black Book" is the name given to the Nevada Gaming Control Board's list of persons not allowed in casinos in the state. Among the first people listed in the "Black Book" was Marshall "Johnny Marshall" Caifano, who sued the state over the legality of the listing. The state's authority was upheld by the U.S. Court of Appeals in 1966.

Q: What hotel's grand opening in 1993 included a spectacular battle between life-size replicas of a pirate ship and a British frigate and the destruction of the Dunes Hotel?

A: The Treasure Island Resort was the site of this memorable duel on October 27, 1993. The two ships, which battle several times daily at the Treasure Island, were rigged to fire shots in the direction of the nearby Dunes. At the correct moment, with loudspeakers relaying the sound of the shots, the venerable Dunes, built in 1955, imploded and crumbled.

Q: How many people are employed in casinos in Nevada?

A: As of 2003, Nevada had 192,812 casino employees.

Q: How many licensed casinos are in Nevada?

A: In 2003, there were 418 casinos in the state with non-restricted gambling licenses, which allow them to have 16 or more slot machines and table games. There are 2,183 casino operators with restricted licenses.

Q: What percentage of Nevada's statewide gambling revenues comes from slot machines versus table games?

A: About 75 percent of statewide gambling revenues come from slot machines, while the remaining 25 percent was from table games, such as poker, baccarat and blackjack.

Downtown Reno
Photo by Reno News Bureau

Q: Where can you find the world's largest, tallest free-standing sign?

A: In 1997, the Las Vegas Hilton erected the world's largest, tallest free-standing sign. It stands twenty-stories high (279 feet) and features more than 6 miles of neon and fluorescent lights. The $9 million sign has a total surface area of 70,100 square feet and is 164-feet wide.

Q: What Las Vegas hotel was the site of a tragic 1980 fire that killed eighty-four people?

A: The former MGM Hotel-Casino (not the same as the MGM Grand Hotel and Theme Park, which was built in 1993) was the site of the fire on November 21, 1980. Following the disaster, the state enacted fire safety regulations that are among the strictest in the nation.

Q: What was the name of the short-lived Las Vegas hotel-casino that was the first racially integrated resort in Nevada?

A: The Moulin Rouge Hotel and Casino, which operated from May to October 1955, was the first club to break the color barrier in Las Vegas. Regrettably, prior to 1960, African-Americans were not allowed to gamble, dine or stay at Las Vegas resorts— except during the brief time the Moulin Rouge was open.

Q: What Lake Tahoe hotel-casino was blown up by a bomb in 1980?

A: Harvey's Resort was destroyed in August 1980 by a bomb placed in the hotel by extortionists. The property, which opened in 1944, was later rebuilt and reopened with six hundred fifty-five rooms. It is the largest hotel-casino at Lake Tahoe.

Q: What kind of business did gaming magnate William Harrah first operate in Reno?

A: Harrah opened a small bingo parlor in Reno in 1937. In 1942, he opened Harrah's Club on Virginia Street in Reno, later adding a hotel and expanding it to cover much of two city blocks.

Q: True or false. Nevada is the only state with legalized prostitution?

A: True. Nevada state law allows brothels to be licensed to operate in counties with a population of 400,000 people or less, meaning it is illegal only in Clark (Las Vegas) and Washoe (Reno) Counties. Smaller counties, however, do have the right to restrict or prohibit prostitution.

Q: Where do the UNLV Runnin' Rebels play basketball?

A: The Rebels, who won the NCAA basketball championship in 1990, play at the Thomas and Mack Center in Las Vegas.

Q: What silent screen actress, who appeared with Charlie Chaplin in *The Tramp* was born and raised in Nevada?

A: Actress Edna Purviance was born in 1896 in Paradise Valley and raised in Lovelock. She starred in nearly forty films with Chaplin and one solo picture before retiring in 1924. She died in Los Angeles in 1958.

Q: In what motion picture, partially filmed at the Nevada State Prison in Carson City, did actor Tom Selleck play an architect unjustly accused of drug possession and sent to prison?

A: The movie was *An Innocent Man* released in 1989.

Q: What was the name of actor John Wayne's last movie, which was filmed in Carson City?

A: John Wayne's final performance was in *The Shootist*, released in 1976.

Q: What 1930s movie star died in an airplane crash near Las Vegas in 1942?

A: Actress Carole Lombard perished in 1942 when the plane carrying her collided with Mount Potosi. Lombard was married to Clark Gable at the time.

Q: Pyramid Lake appeared as what body of water in the movie, *The Greatest Story Ever Told*?

A: Pyramid Lake served as the Sea of Galilee.

Q: In the film, *Total Recall*, what Nevada state park appeared as the harsh environment on the planet Mars?

A: The starkly beautiful Valley of Fire State Park was Mars in the movie, which starred Arnold Schwarzenegger.

Q: Where was much of the aerial photography in the movie, *Top Gun* filmed?

A: While the movie took place in the San Diego area, most of the impressive flying scenes were filmed high above the Fallon Naval Air Station in Nevada.

Q: In 1988, what movie became the first motion picture filmed mostly in Nevada to win an Oscar for Best Picture?

A: The film was *Rain Man*, starring Tom Cruise and Dustin Hoffman.

Q: What movie, partially filmed in Genoa and Carson City, told the story of a writer held captive by a crazed fan?

A: The 1990 film was *Misery* and starred James Caan and Kathy Bates, who won an Academy Award for her performance as the insane fan. While most of the movie was shot on Clear Creek Road, south of Carson City, it was called Colorado in the film.

Q: Who was sitting in the front row when the Beatles made their first appearance in Las Vegas in August 1964?

A: White-bread pop crooner Pat Boone.

The Liberace Museum
Photo courtesy of Las Vegas News Bureau

Q: In what 1967 western movie did the Valley of Fire State Park appear as a stand-in for Mexico?

A: The Valley of Fire served as Mexico in the film, *The Professionals*, which starred Lee Marvin and Jack Palance.

Q: What flamboyant piano player has a museum filled with his collection of cars, capes and candelabra in Las Vegas?

A: The Liberace Museum in Las Vegas celebrates the life and times of famed entertainer Wladziu Valentino Liberace (1919–1987). The museum is chock-full of costumes, jewelry and other mementos collected by the performer. Proceeds from the museum benefit a music scholarship fund created by Liberace.

Q: What singing superstar made her Las Vegas debut at the Riviera Hotel in 1963 as the opening act for Liberace?

A: Barbra Streisand.

Q: What was the first feature film made in Nevada?

A: The first film was *Moving Pictures of Tonopah* made in Tonopah in February and March 1913. Among those appearing in this silent flick were Governor Tasker Oddie and Jim Butler, founder of Tonopah.

Q: What HBO original movie used the Stead Airport north of Reno as both Israel and Iraq, with Pyramid Lake serving as the Dead Sea?

A: The film was *Steal the Sky*, starring Mariel Hemingway and Ben Cross.

Q: In what Sylvester Stallone movie, filmed in Las Vegas, does he play a competitive arm-wrestler trying to earn the love of his son?

A: *Over the Top*, released in 1987, was the film.

Q: What 1961 motion picture, filmed in the Black Rock Desert, Reno and Dayton, was the last movie ever made by both Marilyn Monroe and Clark Gable?

A: *The Misfits* was the name of this film about cowboys hunting wild mustangs. Both Monroe and Gable died shortly after it was released.

Q: What 1980 film told the story of a Nevada trucker who finds Howard Hughes wandering in the desert?

A: The movie was *Melvin and Howard*, starring Jason Robards as the reclusive millionaire and Paul Le Mat as Melvin Dummar. Mary Steenburgen, who portrayed Melvin's wife, Lynda, won an Academy Award.

Q: Which Rocky movie included a fight in Las Vegas between Rocky Balboa pal, Apollo Creed, and Soviet superman, Ivan Drago?

A: This brutal battle, during which Creed (Carl Weathers) died, was *Rocky IV*.

Q: What surrealistic film, set in Las Vegas—but filmed entirely in a Hollywood studio—is about a travel agent (Teri Garr) seeking romance and adventure beyond that offered by her boyfriend (Frederic Forrest), who owns a junkyard?

A: *One From the Heart* was directed by Francis Ford Coppola and released in 1982.

Q: In what 1989 Clint Eastwood flick, partially filmed in Carson City and Reno, did the actor portray a skip tracer searching for a bail-jumping Bernadette Peters?

A: The movie was *Pink Cadillac*.

Q: In what 1984 film did an alien use his extraterrestrial powers to win enough money in Las Vegas casinos to purchase a car so he could drive to a rendezvous with his homebound spaceship?

A: This enchanting film was *Starman*, starring Jeff Bridges.

Q: What t.v. western, which was set in Nevada in the late nineteenth century, followed the adventures of the Cartwright family?

A: *Bonanza* ran from 1959 to 1973, starring Lorne Green, Michael Landon and Dan Blocker. The show has had two revivals; a made-for-t.v. movie in 1987 entitled *Bonanza—The Next Generation*, and a 1993 TV-movie, *Bonanza—The Return*.

Q: What television series starred actor Robert Urich as a Las Vegas private detective?

A: The show, which ran from 1978 to 1981, was called *Vega$* and Urich portrayed Dan Tanna.

Q: What 1980s television show was set in Las Vegas in the 1950s?

A: *Crime Story* was a stylish cops-and-robbers show that attempted to show the infiltration of organized crime in Las Vegas.

Q: What short-lived TV crime show depicted the activities of a team of Las Vegas undercover police officers who dressed as ninjas?

A: The show, which ran in 1988 to 1989, was called *Nasty Boys*.

Q: What is the nation's largest casino company?

A: In 2005, Harrah's, which is headquartered in Las Vegas, was set to become the nation's largest gaming company, with more than 50 casinos nationwide. In mid-2004, Caesars agreed to merge with Harrah's to create a gaming corporation with more than $8 billion in revenues. The deal followed an earlier announced merger between MGM Mirage and Mandalay Bay Resort Group, which together own 28 properties with annual revenues of about $5 billion.

Q: About how many hotel and motel rooms are in Las Vegas?

A: In 2003, there were more than 130,000 hotel and motel rooms in the city.

Q: How many slot machines are in Clark County (Las Vegas area)?

A: Nearly 150,000—or about one for every nine people in the county.

Q: What golfing superstar won his first professional golf tournament in Las Vegas in 1996?

A: Tiger Woods, who won the Las Vegas Invitational on October 6, 1996.

Q: What professional tennis player, winner of more than 47 singles titles, including Wimbledon, was born in Las Vegas?

A: Andre Agassi, born in 1970.

Q: What actor, who played Officer Frank Smith on the *Dragnet* television series from 1953 to 1959, was born in a Nevada settlement that is now a ghost town?

A: Ben Alexander was born in Garfield, Nevada (located near Mina in central Nevada) in 1911. Alexander, who died in 1969, also appeared in the film, *All Quiet on the Western Front* in 1930.

Q: What actor was married in Las Vegas in 1942, 1944, 1948, 1952, 1959, 1967, 1969 and 1978?

A: Mickey Rooney. The oft-wedded performer married Ava Gardner in 1942, Betty Jane Rase in 1944, Martha Vickers in 1948, Elaine Mahnsen in 1952, Barbara Thomason in 1959, Marge Lane in 1967, Carolyn Hockette in 1969 and January Chamberlin in 1978.

Q: What famous cinema *Tarzan* was married in Las Vegas in 1933?

A: Johnny Weissmuller, who married Lupe Velez that year.

Q: What Tony Award-winning Broadway musical comedy is set in the mythical Nevada town of Deadrock?

A: *Crazy For You*, which won three Tony awards in 1992, including Best Musical.

Q: What 1992 film set in Reno starred Whoopie Goldberg as a lounge singer hiding in a convent?

A: *Sister Act*.

Q: What 1996 comedy starring Woody Harrelson and Bill Murray was partially filmed at Reno's National Bowling Stadium?

A: The film was *Kingpin*.

Q: What 1996 blockbuster about an alien invasion was partially filmed at Wendover?

A: *Independence Day*, which starred Jeff Goldblum and Will Smith.

Q: What 1996 flick featured aliens blowing up the Landmark Hotel in Las Vegas?

A: *Mars Attacks*, which featured Jack Nicholson.

Q: What probable future Baseball Hall-of-Fame pitcher, winner of four Cy Young awards in the 1990s, attended high school in Las Vegas and still makes his home there?

A: Greg Maddux of the Atlanta Braves, who attended Valley High.

Q: Who was the first African-American woman to receive a gaming license in Nevada?

A: Sarann Knight-Preddy was the first when she was licensed in 1950.

Q: Who was the first African-American performer to headline at a major Nevada hotel?

A: While other African-American entertainers had previously appeared in Nevada, including the Mills Brothers at the Nevada Biltmore in 1946, singer Lena Horne was the first to headline at one of the large hotels when she appeared at the Flamingo in January 1947.

MINING LORE
Untold Wealth Lost and Found

❖❖❖❖❖❖❖❖❖❖❖❖❖❖❖❖❖❖❖❖❖❖

Q: When was gold discovered in Nevada?

A: In the spring of 1849, prospecting parties from California discovered gold on the eastern slope of the Sierra Nevada Range. The following year, emigrants traveling to California discovered gold nuggets at the mouth of Gold Canyon, near present-day Dayton.

Q: What Virginia City railroad was considered one of the most lucrative short lines in the country?

A: Nearly all of the ore from the Comstock region's fabulous mines was carried on the Virginia & Truckee Railroad, established by William C. Ralston, William Sharon and D. O. Mills. Construction started in February 1869, expanded along the Carson River to Carson City and reached Reno in August 1872. By 1875, between eighty and one hundred carloads of ore were departing daily from Virginia City. The line operated until 1950.

Q: What was the name of the massive gold and silver strike— considered the largest single gold and silver ore pocket ever discovered—that was made on the Comstock Lode in 1873?

A: This major find was called the "Big Bonanza" and yielded more than $100 million over a six-year period.

Q: What colorful mining figure is credited with naming Virginia City?

A: A native of the state of Virginia, James "Old Virginny" Finney, allegedly stumbled and broke a bottle of whiskey on a dirt street in the mining camp developing on the slopes of Mount Davidson. He promptly christened the new community, "Virginia City."

Q: In the 1860s to 1870s, by what name were William C. Ralston, William Sharon and their allies at the Bank of California known?

A: Ralston, Sharon and the bank were commonly called the "Bank Crowd." From 1867 to 1875, the Bank Crowd owned a near monopoly on Virginia City's mills and mines.

Q: Who were the "Bonanza Kings" who controlled the Comstock mining interests from 1875 to 1895?

A: The Bonanza Kings were John W. Mackay, James G. Fair, James C. Flood and William S. O'Brien. These four wrestled control of the Comstock's most productive mines from the Bank Crowd and established their own milling monopoly.

Q: What mineral was king in the Ely region for more than eighty years?

A: Copper was the top mineral produced in Ely's mines, which, from 1900 to the early 1980s, generated more than $1 billion.

Q: What short-lived eastern Nevada mining town's economy was based on marble rather than gold and silver?

A: The camp of Carrera, named for the famed Italian marble district, was founded in 1911 to develop significant marble deposits discovered in a canyon southeast of Beatty. The marble's quality, however, was marginal and the town disappeared by the 1930s.

Sutro Tunnel

Q: Who constructed a horizontal four-mile tunnel that started deep beneath the Comstock mines and ended at a spot just east of Dayton?

A: This engineering marvel, which allowed the Comstock mines to be drained of their dangerous hot water, was designed and built by Adolph Sutro. The tunnel project was started in 1869, despite considerable opposition from the "Bank Crowd" who feared it would eliminate their monopoly. It was finished in 1878 and cost about $3.5 million. Shortly after its completion, Sutro sold his interest in the tunnel for about $1 million—it never made money for its other investors—and became extremely wealthy investing in San Francisco real estate.

Q: What two brothers are credited with first identifying the existence of the rich silver deposits that would later spark the Comstock Lode mining boom?

A: Hosea and Ethan Allen Grosh discovered a rich ledge of silver, which they called the "monster ledge" in 1857 near Gold Canyon. Tragically, neither profited from the discovery. In August 1857, Hosea struck his foot with a pick and died from the injury on September 2, 1857. Later that winter, Ethan Allen became stranded in a snowstorm. Although suffering from severe frostbite in his legs, he refused amputation and died on December 19, 1857.

Q: What two miners are credited with discovering the famed Comstock Lode?

A: While Hosea and Ethan Allen Grosh first identified the existence of silver deposits in the area in 1856, it wasn't until June 1859, when Patrick McLaughlin and Peter O'Riley discovered a solid ledge of silver and gold that the "Rush to Washoe," as the boom was called, began in earnest.

Q: From whom did the rich Comstock Lode take its name?

A: The lode was named after Henry Comstock, a miner who said he had title to the land on which Patrick McLaughlin and Peter O'Riley had made their discovery. To avoid a conflict, McLaughlin and O'Riley agreed to be partners with Comstock, whose name was forevermore linked to the rich lode.

Q: What Nevada mining town was called the "Pittsburgh of the West" because of the heavy smoke belching out its many smelters?

A: Eureka earned this dubious distinction between 1869 and 1872, when sixteen smelters were operating in the area.

Q: Who invented the ingenious method of timbering Virginia City's mines, which allowed greater stability and safety for the underground mines?

A: In November 1860 German engineer Philip Deidesheimer developed the method known as square-set timbering that created a safe and efficient method for removing ore. The basic idea was to construct a system of timbers framed in rectangular sets that could be joined in interlocking cubes and extended in any direction. The design was far more stable than traditional timbering and allowed for the maximum development of Virginia City's mines.

Q: What catastrophic event destroyed nearly all of Virginia City in October 1875?

A: The Great Fire of 1875, started in a small boarding house, destroyed the entire central part of the city. The fire caused an estimated $10 million in damage. While many of the city's homes and businesses were rebuilt, the fire coincided with the beginning of the decline of the Comstock mines, which limited resources for the town's reconstruction.

Q: What was Nevada's second most productive mining region in the nineteenth century, after Virginia City?

A: The second largest producer was Eureka. Lead and silver were discovered in this central Nevada area in 1864, with large-scale mining underway after 1870. By 1878, it had become Nevada's second largest city with more than 9,000 residents.

Q: Where and when was Nevada's first miners' union formed?

A: Nevada's first miners' union was founded on December 8, 1866, in Gold Hill, near Virginia City. It was the first formed west of the Mississippi.

Tonopah
Photo courtesy of Nevada Department of Transportation

Q: In what year did the Tonopah mining boom begin?

A: In May 1900, rancher and occasional miner, Jim Butler, discovered rich silver deposits in Tonopah, sparking a major mining strike that propelled the state into a new period of prosperity.

Q: What early twentieth century central Nevada mining town hotel was once the most luxurious hotel between San Francisco and Denver?

A: This once magnificent inn was the Goldfield Hotel, built in 1908. The four-story brick hotel, still standing but vacant, originally had crystal chandeliers, a solid mahogany lobby and one of the first electric elevators in the state.

Q: True or False—In the 1860s, Virginia City's miners were the highest paid miners in the world?

A: True. In 1866, the average Virginia City miner made $28 per week compared with $4 to $5 per week for miners in Cornwall, England and other parts of the world.

Q: What was the popular name of the international labor union group that struggled to unionize the Goldfield area mines in 1907?

A: The International Workers of the World (IWW), also called the "Wobblies," attempted to organize miners in Goldfield in mid-1907. After the IWW had called a series of strikes, U.S. troops were brought in by President Theodore Roosevelt on December 6, 1907, to bring calm to the city, then were withdrawn on March 6, 1908, and replaced by state police.

Q: What northeastern Nevada mining town was named after a North Carolina Indian tribe?

A: The town of Tuscarora, located north of Elko, was named by John Beard, a pioneering settler in the area, after a famous tribe from his home state of North Carolina.

Austin

Q: When was silver discovered in the central Nevada mining town of Austin?

A: On May 2, 1862, William Talcott, a former Pony Express rider working for the Overland Stagecoach Company, discovered silver in Pony Canyon, a short distance from Jacob's Station in central Nevada. Called the Reese River Mining District, thousands of miners flocked to the area within a year and the town of Austin was established in September 1863.

Q: What was the name of Austin's imaginary nineteenth-century social club that made prevarication an art form?

A: The Sazerac Lying Club was the name of this fictional club, created in the pages of Austin's *Reese River Reveille* in 1873. The escapades of the club appeared in the paper, courtesy of editor Fred Hart, until 1878.

Q: In what town did young Samuel Clemens (Mark Twain) work as a prospector?

A: Clemens arrived in the mining camp of Unionville in late December 1861. He quickly tired of the backbreaking work and after only about two weeks of prospecting, returned to his brother's home in Carson City.

Q: At what Virginia City newspaper did Samuel Clemens assume the nom de plume Mark Twain?

A: Clemens joined the staff of the *Territorial Enterprise* newspaper in September 1862 and started writing under the name, Mark Twain, in January 1863. The origin of his pseudonym has a couple of versions, including several different versions told by Twain. The name was taken from a deceased New Orleans writer; was related to the way depth was measured by Mississippi riverboat pilots; or was derived from the unique shorthand for keeping track of drinks bought on credit at a Virginia City bar.

Q: Where did the first lode mining in Nevada take place?

A: The first lode mining occurred at Potosi, twenty-five miles southwest of Las Vegas, in 1856—a few years before serious rock mining occurred in Virginia City, although placer mining had started earlier in Virginia City.

Q: Where was the location of the second major mining strike of the early twentieth century?

A: The second big mining boom of the twentieth century happened thirty miles south of Tonopah in Goldfield. In December 1902, Harry Stimler and William Marsh discovered rich gold reserves on Columbia Mountain. Within a few years, Goldfield was the largest city in Nevada, with nearly 20,000 residents. The mines began to decline by 1911 and large portions of the town were destroyed by floods and fires in later years. Only a few hundred people live in Goldfield today.

Q: What community, noted for its hot springs, was named after a town in India?

A: Golconda, located east of Winnemucca, was named after the capital city ruled by India's Kutb Shahi dynasty from 1512 to 1687. A popular hot water spa and hotel operated in the town for the first half of the twentieth century.

Q: What Nevada mining town was optimistically named after the legendary king with the golden touch?

A: Early gold ore samples from an area in northern Elko County indicated such wealth that miners called it the Midas Mining District. Midas, however, proved a bit disappointing and never measured up to its name.

Q: What name did many Nevada miners, particularly those of Cornish background, give to the mischievous elf or troll-like creatures who allegedly warned of disasters and mishaps in the mines?

A: These impish creatures were called "Tommyknockers." They supposedly made tapping sounds to indicate the location of rich ore as well as to warn of coming disaster. Tommyknockers also played pranks on the miners, like dropping small rocks on their heads or taking tools.

Q: What other names did the mining town of Gold Point assume to reflect the fact it was producing more of other deposits?

A: The town of Lime Point, founded in 1868, was named after its lime deposits. In 1905 the town changed its name to Hornsilver after significant silver discoveries were made. Then in 1930 it became Gold Point because it was producing far more gold than silver.

Gold Point

Q: What was the unusual name given to the Austin City Railway's steam locomotive?

A: Operating on a steep 2.8-mile rail line that ran between Austin and Clifton, the locomotive was named "Mules' Relief," because it replaced an earlier mule-power operation. The train ran from 1882 to 1889.

Q: What was the name of the prospector who became lost near Death Valley, stumbled upon some exceptionally valuable ore, then could not remember the location of his strike?

A: This unlucky man was named Charles C. Breyfogle and his discovery, in 1864, became known as the "Lost Breyfogle Mine." While some believe he discovered Goldfield (about a half century before anyone else had), others insist the mine is still out there awaiting rediscovery.

Q: What Virginia City miner, who was probably the first Comstock millionaire, built a magnificent mansion in Washoe Valley that is today a county park?

A: Lemuel "Sandy" Bowers is considered the Comstock's first millionaire. With his wife, Eilley, he owned twenty feet of the richest surface ore deposits on the Comstock Lode. In 1864, the two built a fabulous sandstone mansion in Washoe Valley and stocked it with imported furnishings. In 1868, Sandy Bowers died and his wife lost the mansion in 1876 to creditors. In 1946, it was sold to Washoe County and restored to its original condition in 1967.

Q: What mining town is named for an investor who owned most of the mining claims in the area, but never visited the town?

A: The eastern Nevada town of Pioche is named after Francois Pioche, a San Francisco financier, who, in 1869, bought several claims and paid to erect a smelter. In 1870, a town was platted and named after Pioche, who never visited his investment.

Q: Why was Pioche considered one of Nevada's roughest towns?

A: Because of its remote location, more than 400 miles from more populous western Nevada, Pioche had little in the way of law enforcement. As a result, nearly sixty percent of the state's killings in 1871 to 1872, occurred in Pioche.

Q: What southern Nevada mining community on the edge of Death Valley once served as the intersection of three separate railroad lines?

A: Following gold discoveries in 1904, by 1907, Rhyolite was served by the Las Vegas & Tonopah, the Tonopah & Tidewater and the Bullfrog-Goldfield Railroads. At the time, the boomtown had more than 6,000 residents as well as newspapers, a stock exchange, banks and schools. The area's mines proved to be less productive than originally believed and the town experienced a rapid decline. By 1920, only fourteen people remained and Rhyolite was on its way to becoming a ghost town. Today, no one lives there.

Rhyolite

Q: What was the foreboding nickname of the mining town of Delamar?

A: Delamar was frequently called "The Widow Maker" because dry drilling in the town's mines created clouds of silica dust, which caused fatal silicosis.

Q: What mining town, originally called Teel's Marsh, was the site of Francis "Borax" Smith's first major success as a borax miner?

A: Marietta helped launch the career of Borax Smith. Smith and his brother began mining in Marietta in 1872, founding the Teel's Marsh Borax Company, which later became the Pacific Borax Salt & Soda Company. The town was abandoned in the 1890s. Smith later had great success mining borax in Death Valley.

Q: What did Austin shop owner Reuel Gridley do in 1864 after losing a bet on the outcome of an election that year?

A: Gridley carried a fifty-pound sack of flour a distance of a mile and a quarter through the town. Following the procession, Gridley auctioned the sack, with the proceeds donated to the Sanitary Fund, which was the predecessor to the Red Cross. The sack was resold several times that day, generating nearly $5,000 for the Sanitary Fund. Word of Gridley's famed sack of flour spread and he was invited to communities throughout the West to hold charity auctions of the sack. He ultimately raised nearly a quarter of a million dollars for the Sanitary Fund.

Q: What did Austin's city fathers do to help attract a railroad to the town?

A: In 1880, Austin was so eager to have a railroad that its city council extended the town's limits by one mile to help the Nevada Central Railroad qualify for a $200,000 state subsidy. In 1869, the state granted a charter to the Nevada Central that would result in a subsidy of $200,000, if a rail line could be connected to the Austin city limits prior to midnight, February 9, 1880. The railroad dawdled for years, then, with seven months remaining on the charter, began construction. After months of frantic work, the railroad was a mile and a half short of the town with six hours until deadline. The Austin City Council came to its rescue, agreeing to extend the city limit one mile toward the rail line. The last half-mile was completed by volunteers from the town, who helped to lay the tracks—without wood ties—until they were ten feet within the new city limits. The job was done with ten minutes to spare.

Q: What mining town was called Dixie until a majority of the residents favored the other side in the Civil War?

A: The northern Nevada town of Unionville switched sides in 1861, when Northern sympathizers outnumbered Confederates and changed the name to reflect their political beliefs.

Q: What was the name of the famed opera singer who was raised in the mining town of Austin and performed throughout Europe and America in the 1880s and '90s?

A: Emma Wixom, who sang under the stage name, Emma Nevada, was born in 1860 in northern California and moved to Austin at the age of four. She made her first public appearance as a singer at an Austin church at the age of ten. In 1873, she was enrolled at Mills Seminary near Oakland and began her formal music training. In the mid-1870s, she moved to Paris for additional training and embarked on her successful career. She died in England in 1940.

Q: What well-traveled hotel was originally located in Virginia City, then moved to Austin in 1863?

A: The International Hotel was originally built in Virginia City in the early 1860s, then moved to Austin in 1863. It burned in 1873 and was rebuilt. Portions of that building remain standing.

Esmeralda County Courthouse, Goldfield

Q: What mining town courthouse boasts original Tiffany lamps?

A: The Esmeralda County Courthouse in Goldfield has a set of original Tiffany lamps, installed in 1908. The crystal lamps were an indication of the incredible wealth once found in this mining town.

Q: What southern Nevada mining town is popularly thought to have been named after a brand of sulphur matches?

A: The town of Searchlight, sixty miles south of Las Vegas, is frequently reported as having been named for a pack of Searchlight brand matches. Some historians, however, credit the name to a humorous comment made by one of the town's founders, a prospector named George F. Colton, who allegedly said it would take a searchlight to find much gold in the area.

Q: What Nevada mining town was originally named Grandpa?

A: Goldfield was originally called Grandpa because the gold strike made there was thought to be so big it was the granddaddy of all mining discoveries.

Q: What was the name of the eastern Nevada railroad founded in 1905 to transport ore from Ely area copper mines to the Southern Pacific Railroad line located 140 miles to the north?

A: This short line was named the Nevada Northern Railway and it operated from 1905 until 1983. In the late 1980s, a portion of the route was reopened as a tourist excursion railroad.

Q: What was the name of the infamous 1860s Austin stock scam?

A: The fraudulent Reese River Navigation Company sold stock shares to capitalize a fleet of barges to carry Austin ore on the Reese River. The river, unfortunately, is little more than a creek and rarely deep or wide enough to float a rowboat.

Q: What mining town was named after a Roman Catholic holiday, yet never had a church?

A: The central Nevada town of Candelaria gained its name from a mining claim established in 1865 by Spanish explorers. The name derives from the Catholic holiday of Candlemas Day. Despite growing to about 1,500 residents in 1881, the town never built a church.

Stokes Castle

Q: What is the name given to the summer home that mining millionaire Anson P. Stokes built on a hillside over-looking the Reese River Valley (near Austin)?

A: This unique three-story stone tower, designed after an Italian villa that Stokes fancied, is called "Stokes Castle." The tall, narrow building was completed in 1897, but only used for a couple of years.

Q: What was responsible for the unusual name given to the mining camp of Bullfrog?

A: The town was named for the green-colored rock in which gold was originally discovered in 1904. The green rock reminded Frank "Shorty" Harris and Eddie Cross, the area's first successful prospectors, of a bullfrog's coloring.

Site of Bullfrog

Q: What landmark building was originally located in the mining town of Belmont, then was moved in 1908 to Manhattan?

A: The Catholic Church in Manhattan was originally built in nearby Belmont in 1874. In 1901, the church was effectively abandoned in Belmont, then, in 1908, moved to Manhattan, about fifteen miles away.

Original Belmont Catholic Church

Q: What audacious mining town, now gone, once offered $50,000 to state leaders to move the territorial capital there?

A: In 1864, American Flat (also called American City) offered $50,000 to state leaders to move the territorial capital there from Carson City. The town, located south of Gold Hill, however, never grew to more than a few hundred people. The town disappeared by the late 1920s, despite being the location of the world's largest cyanide plant, built in 1920.

Ruins at American Flat

Q: In the courthouse of what former mining town did convicted murderer Charles Manson carve his initials?

A: Manson scratched his initials into a wall of the Belmont Courthouse, now a state park.

Ward Charcoal Ovens
Photo courtesy of Nevada Department of Transportation

Q: What unique, beehive-shaped structures are found south of Ely?

A: These unusual stone domes are the Ward Charcoal Ovens, built in 1876 to produce charcoal for the smelters in the Ward Mining District, located about twenty miles south of Ely. There are six ovens, each measuring about thirty-five feet high.

GEOGRAPHY
Places and the People Who Made Them
❖❖❖❖❖❖❖❖❖❖❖❖❖❖❖❖❖❖❖❖❖

Q: What does the word "Nevada" mean?

A: The state's name translates as "snow-capped" in Spanish. Although it is one of the driest states, Nevada includes the Sierra Nevadas ("snow-capped mountains").

Q: What is the highest point in Nevada ?

A: Boundary Peak in the White Mountain Range on the California-Nevada border is 13,143 feet high.

Q: What Nevada peak was originally called "mountain which fell in upon itself" by the native Paiutes of northern Nevada?

A: The aptly named Slide Mountain, located above Washoe Valley, south of Reno, earned its name because of the dramatic partially collapsed profile on its southeast face, caused by numerous rock slides.

Q: What is Nevada's state capital?

A: Carson City, located thirty-five miles south of Reno, in northwestern Nevada.

Q: How was the name Carson City derived?

A: Carson City was named after the Carson River, which flowed through the area. The river, in turn, was named in 1844 by John C. Fremont in honor of his scout, Kit Carson.

State Capital Building in Carson City

Q: What color is the dome of Nevada's State Capital?

A: The dome is silver to commemorate the importance this precious metal played in the state's development.

Q: What river's name was originally Sandwich Island River, then was changed to reflect the current name of the Sandwich Islands?

A: The Owyhee River was originally named by explorer Peter Skene Ogden and other trappers for the Sandwich Islands because some natives of those islands were killed by Indians at the river's mouth. When the Sandwich Islands became "Hawaii," the river's name was also changed on maps but the spelling followed phonetic methods—Owyhee.

Q: Why is the valley in which Carson City is located called Eagle Valley?

A: Shortly after opening the first trading post in the area, Frank Hall shot an eagle flying over the post, which he stuffed and mounted on the building, providing the impetus for the name.

Q: Where is Nevada's only winery?

A: The Pahrump Valley Vineyards is located, naturally, in Pahrump, about forty-five miles west of Las Vegas.

Q: What is the current name of the tall mountain that rises above Virginia City, which was originally known as Sun Mountain?

A: Mount Davidson, which is the tallest in Storey County, was named to honor Donald Davidson, state geologist of California, who scaled the mountain in the mid-nineteenth century.

Q: What is Nevada's largest county?

A: Nye County, in central Nevada, with 18,294 square miles is also the third largest county in the nation.

Q: What Nevada town was named for Christopher Columbus' birthplace?

A: Genoa honors Columbus' Italian hometown because one of the town's founders, Orson Hyde, believed the area resembled the Genoa harbor. Nevadans mispronounce the town's name as "jen-NO-ah."

Q: How many tunnels can you drive a car through in Nevada?

A: Four. There are pairs of tunnels at Cave Rock, on the east side of Lake Tahoe and near the Humboldt Palisades on Interstate Highway 80 east of Carlin.

"Million Dollar Courthouse"

Q: Where is the "Million Dollar Courthouse?"

A: This famous courthouse is located in Pioche in eastern Nevada. The two-story stone building received its nickname because it cost nearly a million dollars by the time it was paid for, some sixty-six years later, due to kickbacks, cost overruns and numerous refinancing of debt.

Q: What Nevada highway is called the "Loneliest Road in America?"

A: In 1986, *Life* magazine said drivers needed survival skills to make the trip along the 287-mile portion of U.S. Highway 50 between Ely and Fernley, and dubbed it the "Loneliest Road in America." To capitalize on the publicity, the Nevada legislature officially designated the highway the Loneliest Road in 1987.

Q: For whom was the railroad town of Nixon named?

A: It wasn't the former president, rather this Nixon was named for U.S. Senator George S. Nixon, who served from 1905 until his death in 1912.

Q: What is the name of the valley where Reno is located?

A: The Truckee Meadows

Q: What was the name of the mythical transcontinental river sought by many of Nevada's earliest explorers, including John C. Fremont?

A: San Buenaventura River was believed to be a link between the Atlantic and Pacific Oceans.

Q: In what year did Nevada successfully annex 150 miles of land previously part of Utah and Arizona?

A: In 1866, the U.S. Congress set those boundaries for Nevada in an effort to resolve border disputes among the three states.

Q: What four Nevada counties no longer exist?

A: Lake County once encompassed the northwestern corner of the state (now part of Washoe County). It became known as Roop County in 1862. Roop County was abolished in 1883 because of lack of population. Ormsby County was the previous name for Carson City. Bullfrog County was the name of a short-lived southwestern Nevada county created in the mid-1980s to let the state heavily tax the federal government's proposed Yucca Mountain nuclear waste dump site. It was ruled invalid by the Nevada Supreme Court.

Nevada's Humboldt River
A relatively straight stretch near Winnemucca

Q: What river was originally called Unknown River, then Mary's River?

A: The Humboldt River, which was a key source of water for emigrants traveling across Nevada in the mid-nineteenth century, received its current name in honor of Baron Alexander von Humboldt, a famed nineteenth-century explorer.

Q: How tall is Hoover Dam, which stretches between Nevada and Arizona?

A: Hoover Dam, located south of Las Vegas, is 726.4 feet high. Constructed from 1931 to 1935, it is considered one of the engineering marvels of the world. Built at a cost of $175 million, the dam is 1,244 feet across and contains 3.25 million cubic yards of concrete—enough to pave a two-lane highway from San Francisco to New York. Because it was designed to tame the Colorado River, it is shaped like a giant wedge, with a base in the bedrock that is 660 feet thick.

Hoover Dam
Photo courtesy of Bureau of Reclamation

Q: What major Nevada dam was part of the first ever federal reclamation project?

A: Lahontan Dam, located near the western Nevada community of Fallon, was part of the Newlands Water Project, which was approved in 1902. The earthen dam, which measures about 120 feet high and 1,300 feet wide, was completed in 1914.

Q: What is Nevada's smallest incorporated city?

A: The smallest municipality is Gabbs, located about 140 miles southeast of Reno, in central Nevada. It has 660 people.

Q: What Nevada town was named for an Italian opera composer?

A: Central Pacific Railroad officials named the tiny enclave of Verdi, west of Reno, after composer Giuseppe Verdi. Interestingly, the town's name is mispronounced as "ver-DYE" in Nevada.

Q: What former Nevada mining town was once simultaneously considered the seat of two counties, in two different states?

A: From 1861 to 1863, Aurora was seat of both Mono County, California, and Esmeralda County, Nevada. The confusion over the town's location was settled in 1863, after both states agreed to a new land survey to resolve the boundary dispute.

Q: What is Nevada's largest law firm?

A: Lionel, Sawyer & Collins, with 85 attorneys.

Q: What are Nevada's three largest incorporated cities?

A: According to the State of Nevada Demographer, in 2003, they are: Las Vegas, with 528,617 residents; Henderson, with 217,448 residents, and Reno with 195,727 residents.

Q: What is Nevada's only consolidated city-county government?

A: Carson City, which changed from Ormsby County in 1969.

Q: How many counties are there in Nevada?

A: There are seventeen counties.

Q: In which Nevada counties do the county seats have the same name as the county?

A: There are three: Carson City, Elko and Eureka Counties.

Q: Which two Nevada counties are named after men who once ran against each other for president of the United States?

A: Lincoln (for President Abraham Lincoln) and Douglas (after his opponent Stephen A. Douglas).

Q: For how many years has the Nevada Day Parade been held in Carson City?

A: The parade, which celebrates Nevada's admission as a state, has been conducted on Nevada Day (October 31) continuously since 1938. Nevada Day was officially declared a state holiday in 1933.

Q: What Nevada community was named after a newspaper comic strip?

A: Jiggs in Elko County was named for the cartoon character of the "Maggie and Jiggs" duo featured in *Bringing Up Father*, a comic strip that started in 1913 and continues to this day. The name was suggested by a local rancher to settle a controversy with postal authorities about what to name the community. It was previously called Dry Creek, then Mound Valley, then Skelton, and then Hylton. The dispute reminded him of the bickering between the comic strip's two protagonists.

Reno Arch
Photo courtesy of Reno News Bureau

Q: How many arches have proclaimed Reno the "Biggest Little City in the World?"

A: Three. The first was constructed in 1926 to celebrate completion of the transcontinental highways, the Lincoln and Victory (and modified in the 1930s to incorporate the city's slogan). It was replaced in 1963 and, again, in 1987. Origins of the slogan vary but most historians believe it was adopted in the 1920s as part of a chamber of commerce promotion.

Q: What city is home of the National Automobile Museum?

A: Reno is the location of this renowned repository of automotive history. The museum has a collection of nearly three hundred unique and historic cars on display.

Q: What major road was originally part of the "Victory Highway?"

A: Interstate Highway 80, across northern Nevada, was originally a portion of the transcontinental Victory Highway, which was then U.S. Highway 40, before becoming part of the interstate highway system.

Q: Where can you find the "Extraterrestrial Highway?"

A: In 1996, Nevada Route 375, between Warm Springs and Hiko, was officially designated the "Extraterrestrial Highway" by the state of Nevada because it borders the so-called "Area 51," allegedly the site of a secret U.S. military base devoted to studying extraterrestrial phenomena.

Q: What Nevada highway was once part of the Lincoln Highway?

A: U.S. Highway 50, which stretches some 300 miles across the middle of the state, was part of the Lincoln Highway, which was the first transcontinental road. Parts of U.S. Highway 50 also parallel the original Pony Express Route and Overland Stage Road.

U.S. Highway 50

Q: What is the longest road in Nevada?

A: The longest road is U.S. Highway 95, which stretches an amazing 665 miles from McDermitt, on the Nevada-Oregon border, to the southern tip of Nevada, at a point about seventy miles south of Las Vegas, where it passes into California.

Q: What is the average elevation in Nevada?

A: The state's average elevation is 5,000 feet, or nearly a mile high.

Q: How many acres of Nevada are designated as wilderness?

A: There are 798,067 acres of designated wilderness in the state, including: Arc Dome (115,000 acres), Jarbidge (113,167 acres), Table Mountain (98,000 acres), Ruby Mountains (90,000 acres), Mount Moriah (82,000 acres), Grant Range (50,000 acres), Mount Charleston (43,000), Alta Toquima (38,000), East Humboldt Range (36,900), Current Mountains (36,000), Santa Rosas (31,000), Mount Rose (28,000), Quinn Canyon (27,000) and Boundary Peak (10,000 acres).

Q: What is the only city in Nevada where gambling is illegal?

A: Officials banned gambling and the sale of alcohol to maintain worker productivity in Boulder City, located twenty-four miles southeast of Las Vegas. The community was founded in 1931 as a company town for workers on the Hoover Dam project. Hard liquor sales were prohibited until 1969.

Q: Where in Nevada will you find that justice isn't blind?

A: The Storey County Courthouse in Virginia City boasts a statue of Lady Justice that isn't wearing a blindfold.

Q: How many people are buried in Hoover Dam?

A: Contrary to myth, no one is buried in the dam. There were one hundred eleven fatalities during the construction of the dam (1931 to 1935).

Pershing County Courthouse
Photo by Ken Evans

Q: Where can you find the only round courthouse in Nevada?
A: The Pershing County Courthouse in Lovelock, built in 1921, is one of only two round courthouses in the country.

Q: Where is the Lexington Arch?
A: This seventy-five-foot high natural limestone arch is located at the southern end of the Great Basin National Park in eastern Nevada.

Virginia City Camel Races
Photo courtesy of Nevada Commission on Tourism

Q: Where can you find the annual International Camel Races?

A: These humorous races, which feature amateur riders atop untrained camels going in every direction, are held each September in Virginia City. The races were started as a joke in 1959—director John Huston was the first winner—and have become world famous.

Q: While changes in the locations of Nevada's county seats were common in the nineteenth and early twentieth centuries, what was the last county to change its seat?

A: Lander County moved its county offices from Austin to Battle Mountain in 1979 because of population shifts.

Reno Air Races
Photo courtesy of Reno News Bureau

Q: Where are the annual National Championship Air Races, Hot August Nights and the Nevada State Fair held?

A: The Biggest Little City, Reno, hosts these unique special events.

Q: What former Nevada railroad camp was named for a directional sign to a saloon?

A: Tobar in northeastern Nevada was named by railroad officials for a directional sign they found in the area that indicated "To bar."

Q: What former Nevada town had an unusually backward name?

A: Adaven, which is Nevada spelled backward, was used by a small settlement in Elko County for a short time in 1916. Later it applied to a town in Nye County, which was served by a post office with that name from May 1, 1939, to November 30, 1953.

Q: Where in Nevada do three U.S. Highways meet?

A: U.S. Highways 50, 93 and 6 all intersect in the eastern Nevada town of Ely.

Q: At what point does U.S. Highway 93, which runs along the state's eastern side, intersect with U.S. Highway 95, which runs along the western side?

A: The two roads meet in Las Vegas, where they also crisscross with Interstate Highway 15.

Q: Where can you find the Nevada State Railroad Museum?

A: This wonderful warehouse of railroad history is located in Carson City.

Q: Where can you find the only wooden courthouse still in use in Nevada?

A: The last wooden hall of justice is the Churchill County Courthouse in Fallon, built in 1903.

Q: Where is the Nevada Northern Railway Museum?

A: Ely is the home of this fine, small museum dedicated to preserving the history and equipment of the Nevada Northern Railway, a short line railroad in eastern Nevada.

"The Ghost Train of Old Ely"
at the Nevada Northern Railway Museum

George W. Ferris

Photo courtesy of Grace Dangberg Foundation

G. W. G. FERRIS

Originator of the Great Ferris Wheel on Midway Plaisance

Q: What famous nineteenth-century inventor/architect was raised in Carson City?

A: George Washington Gale Ferris, Jr., inventor of the Ferris Wheel, lived at 311 West Third Street in Carson City (now called the Ferris House) during his boyhood years. Legend says he was inspired to create his wheel after recalling the waterwheels on the Carson River that were used to crush ore from Virginia City.

Q: What two Nevada communities operate on Mountain standard time rather than Pacific standard time?

A: The border boomtowns of Jackpot, on the Nevada-Idaho boundary, and Wendover, on the Nevada-Utah line, are the only towns that operate in a different time zone.

Q: What is the closest town to the Great Basin National Park?

A: Located five miles from the park, the tiny hamlet of Baker, population about sixty-five, is the nearest community.

Q: True or False, Nevada produced nearly a half-million barrels of oil in 2003?

A: True. In 2003, Nevada produced 493,000 barrels of oil. Most of Nevada's oil resources were produced in two areas, the Railroad Valley region, southwest of Ely, and Pine Valley, south of Carlin.

Q: Near what city is the Red Rock Canyon Recreation Area located?

A: This beautiful natural scenic area is located fifteen miles west of Las Vegas in the Spring Mountains.

Q: What Nevada community was earlier known by the names, Spafford Hall's Station and Chinatown, before assuming its current name?

A: Dayton, located fifteen miles east of Carson City. The town gained its name after 1861, when surveyor John Day platted a town site, which was named Dayton in his honor.

Q: What was the first state office building constructed in Las Vegas?

A: The appropriately-named "State Office Building," also known as the Campos State Office Building, at 215 East Bonanza Road in Las Vegas was the first state office complex. It was built in 1954.

Q: Which mountains boast the only commercial helicopter skiing operation in Nevada?

A: The Ruby Mountains in northeastern Nevada are popular with heli-skiers.

Q: Where can you belly-up to Nevada's oldest bar?

A: The Genoa Bar in the small western Nevada town of Genoa opened in 1863.

Q: How many states touch Nevada?

A: Five: Arizona, California, Idaho, Oregon and Utah.

Q: What historical figures are honored with statues in the small park located between the State Capital and the State Legislative Building in Carson City?

A: Three statues honor the following: Abraham Curry, the "Father of Carson City," who laid out the town site and built many of its buildings; Kit Carson, the trailblazing scout, who traveled with explorer John C. Fremont on an 1844 expedition that opened Nevada to the country; and Adolph Sutro who built the Sutro Tunnel, a four-mile engineering marvel that helped make Virginia City's mines more accessible.

Q: How many of Nevada's existing courthouses were designed by the same architect and what was his name?

A: Famed Reno architect Frederick J. DeLongchamps designed five of the state's courthouses—Carson City, Douglas, Humboldt, Lyon and Washoe Counties. DeLongchamps also designed a sixth, the Clark County Courthouse, built in 1913, but it was demolished in the 1960s.

Q: What Nevada city is sometimes called the "Rose City of the Silver State?"

A: Caliente in eastern Nevada is referred to as the Rose City because of a large rose garden created by a local resident, Thomas F. Dixon, to honor his deceased wife. Additionally, in 1930, Caliente entered a rose-covered float in the Tournament of Roses Parade Pasadena and won a special award.

Q: Where is the National Judicial College?

A: The National Judicial College, which trains jurists from throughout the country in the finer points of the law, is located on the campus of the University of Nevada, Reno.

Q: What is the oldest surviving courthouse building in Nevada?

A: The original Douglas County Courthouse in Genoa, built in 1865, is the oldest hall of justice in the state. It ceased to be used as a courthouse in 1916, when the county seat was moved from Genoa to Minden. The two-story red brick building now houses the Genoa Courthouse Museum.

Q: What is the oldest continuously operated courthouse in Nevada?

A: The Storey County Courthouse in Virginia City, built in 1875, has served as a courthouse longer than any other building in the state.

Q: What state park is located within Carson City limits?

A: The only state park in Carson City's boundaries is Lake Tahoe State Park. While most of the park is located in Washoe County, a portion of the park crosses into Carson City.

Q: What unique status does Carson City's Masonic Lodge have?

A: Founded on February 23, 1862, Lodge #154 (later called Nevada Masonic Lodge #1) was the first Masonic Lodge established between the Rocky Mountains and the Sierra Nevada.

Miners' Union Hall, Virginia City

Q: What community is nicknamed "Queen of the Comstock?"

A: The historic mining town of Virginia City has been called by that name because its fortunes were linked to the mineral wealth of the nearby Comstock Lode.

Q: What northern Nevada roadside community—named after a famous French battle site—was the setting for the cover photo of a 1981 Bruce Springsteen album released in Europe?

A: The rock star apparently was looking for a place that represented the real America and found it at the Valmy Motor Court in the tiny town of Valmy, located between Battle Mountain and Winnemucca.

Q: What famous military precision flying team is headquartered at the Nellis Air Force Base, north of Las Vegas?

A: The Thunderbirds, who perform aerial acrobatics all over the world, consider Nellis home.

Q: What Nevada community was named after a female miner who was known as the "Copper Queen?"

A: The hamlet is Mina, located thirty-four miles south of Hawthorne. It was named in 1905 by officials of the Carson & Colorado Railroad in honor of Ferminia Sarras, a Nicaraguan-born woman of Spanish descent, who owned several successful mines in the region.

Q: What was the name of the Southern Pacific Railroad train that mysteriously crashed near Elko in 1939, killing twenty-four people?

A: The train was the City of San Francisco, a streamliner that jumped the tracks while crossing a bridge over the Humboldt River. While railroad officials declared the accident an act of sabotage, no one was ever arrested. Some witnesses, however, said the derailment was caused by excessive speed and chided the railroad for not accepting responsibility.

Q: The State Capital was built in 1870 to 1871, but the State Legislative Building wasn't constructed until when?

A: The 96,000-square-foot legislative building was completed in 1970.

Q: What was Reno's first public park?

A: Wingfield Park, located on Belle Isle in the Truckee River, was donated to the city of Reno in 1920 by financier George Wingfield.

Lake Mead
Photo by Las Vegas News Bureau

Q: What is the largest man-made lake in Nevada?

A: Lake Mead, created by Hoover Dam, is the largest with a 550-mile shoreline.

Q: For whom was Carson City's largest park, Mills Park, named?

A: The park, bordered by U.S. Highway 50, was named for Darius Ogden Mills, longtime owner of the Virginia & Truckee Railroad (V&T). The fifty-two-acre park was originally known as "Folly's Forest," because of the large cotton-woods growing there. Later, the site became an oil storage center for the V&T Railroad. In 1951, the D. O. Mills estate donated the land (for $10) to Carson City for a park.

Q: What suburb of Las Vegas was once known by the rather plain name of Basic?

A: The city of Henderson, eleven miles southeast of Las Vegas, was originally called Basic because it was adjacent to the massive Basic Magnesium Plant, the first major industrial facility built in southern Nevada. In 1953, the town was incorporated as Henderson, in honor of U.S. Senator Charles Henderson.

Q: Where can you watch the Nevada State Mucking and Drilling Championships?

A: Tonopah's annual Jim Butler Days celebration, held Memorial Day weekend, hosts these competitions. Mucking is a mining term referring to the act of shoveling rock and dirt into an ore cart, while drilling refers to the process of hammering holes in the rock walls of a mine shaft, into which dynamite was placed.

Q: Where in southern Nevada can you find one of the world's tallest roller coaster?

A: In Jean, Nevada, located forty-five miles south of Las Vegas, you can ride on the Desperado at Buffalo Bill's Resort. The roller coaster has a vertical drop of two-hundred twenty-five feet and reaches speeds in excess of eighty miles per hour.

Q: What oddity existed on the official state seal from 1866 to 1913?

A: The original seal depicted a train heading from left to right, with smoke trailing behind it, as well as a smoke-stack, with smoke blowing in the opposite direction—generally a physical impossibility. Since 1913, all smoke on the seal has blown in the same direction. Some historians, however, believe the seal didn't need to be changed since the train's momentum would have pushed the smoke behind it, regardless of the wind's direction.

Q: In what Nevada museum can you see a unique pair of shoes that have two cow hooves on the bottom of each?

A: Elko's Northeastern Nevada Museum has these unusual shoes, which were made by a 1920s cattle rustler known as "Crazy Tex". The shoes were designed to mask Tex's tracks when stealing cows (he even trained himself to walk with the same gait as a cow). A pair of deputies, however, caught Tex in the act. He went to prison and his shoes were placed in the museum.

Q: Where is the geographic center of Nevada?

A: The center of Nevada is located at a spot about twenty-five miles southeast of Austin in the Monitor Valley.

THE FIRST NEVADANS
Indian Culture and Myth

❖❖❖❖❖❖❖❖❖❖❖❖❖❖❖❖❖❖❖❖❖❖❖

Q: What Paiute leader befriended and served as a guide for many of the early explorers across Nevada, including John C. Fremont?

A: Captain Truckee, for whom the Truckee River is named, was a guide for many of the early emigrants crossing the state.

Q: What are the main Indian tribes in Nevada?

A: The main tribes are the Northern Paiutes, the Southern Paiutes, the Shoshones and the Washoes. The Northern Paiutes originally inhabited the area from Walker Lake to Pyramid Lake; the Southern Paiutes lived in the vicinity of Las Vegas and eastern Nevada; the Shoshones resided in the northeastern and central portions of the state; and the Washoes lived in far western Nevada.

Q: By what name do both the Northern Paiutes and Shoshone call whites?

A: Both refer to whites as Taibo, or white people.

Q: By what name were Pyramid Lake Paiutes known?

A: The tribes living around Pyramid Lake were known as the Kuyuidikado, meaning the cui-ui eaters or fish eaters.

Q: By what name did Northern Paiutes call their rounded huts constructed of woven cattails and rushes?

A: These traditional Paiute dwellings were called karnees.

Winnemucca
Photo courtesy of Nevada Historical Society

Q: What Paiute chief led his people throughout the period of white settlement in Nevada in the 1850s and 1860s?

A: Old Winnemucca, also called Poito, was born in the 1790s. He lived through the arrival of the whites, the loss of Indian lands, and other devastating changes to his culture and died in 1882.

Q: By what name do the Northern Paiutes call themselves?

A: The Northern Paiutes call themselves the Numa, meaning the people.

Q: What does pogonip mean?

A: Pogonip is the Shoshonean word describing the frosty, morning fog that often occurs in northern Nevada during the winter. It translates as "white death," because it was believed to cause pneumonia.

Q: What is the significance of the word, "pah" and why does it appear in so many Nevada place names?

A: Pah is the Southern Paiute word for "water." Since water was so scarce in early Nevada, communities generally formed near places where water was found. Frequently, these areas or towns would adopt the native name for the place, which usually contained some reference to water.

Q: What is the only city in Nevada named for a Native American?

A: French Ford was renamed Winnemucca in 1866 by officials of the Central Pacific Railroad in honor of the famous Indian chief.

Q: What is the largest Indian reservation in Nevada?

A: With nearly a half-million acres, the Pyramid Lake Reservation is the largest. It is also the oldest, having been set aside in 1859 and legally recognized by the U.S. government in 1874.

Q: Who was the first Native American elected to the Nevada legislature?

A: Dewey E. Sampson of Reno was elected to the Nevada State Assembly in 1939 and served one term. He is the only Native American to have ever served in the legislature.

Petroglyphs

Q: What name is given to the prehistoric rock writings found throughout Nevada?

A: These unique writings found carved in rocks and cliff walls are called petroglyphs. Most are believed to date from 800 B.C. to about A.D. 1200. Many scholars believe they were part of tribal rituals related to religious observances or hunting.

Q: What crop does the Duckwater Indian tribe grow in warm water ponds?

A: The tribe, which lives about seventy miles southeast of Ely, raises delicious catfish, which is sold to many restaurants in Nevada.

Q: In what cave near Fallon have archaeologists found valuable artifacts?

A: Hidden Cave is a treasure trove of pots, nets, baskets and other objects that help in the understanding of early Native American society and the geological history of the region. It was discovered in the 1930s, and excavated several times in the intervening years (most recently in 1979 to 1980).

Q: What mythical creature is believed to live in Walker Lake?

A: Over the years, there have been a number of reports of a sea serpent in Walker Lake. The native Walker River Paiutes have long believed in the existence of giant serpents in the lake, located near Hawthorne. According to the Walker River Paiute tribal history, two serpents live in the lake, a male and a female, and children were told not to make fun of them or talk lightly about them.

Q: What is the name given to the prehistoric Indians who lived in the West, including Nevada, prior to the modern tribes?

A: Prehistoric people called the Anasazi ("Ancient Ones"), or Pueblo people, are believed to have lived in the region nine hundred to one thousand five hundred to years ago.

Q: What is the only Nevada county with a Native American name?

A: Washoe County in northwestern Nevada is derived from a Native American word. Washoe refers to the tribe, also spelled Washo, that once roamed most of far western Nevada.

Sarah Winnemucca Hopkins
Photo courtesy of Nevada Historical Society

Q: Who wrote the landmark work, *Life among the Piutes: Their Wrongs and Claims*, in 1883?

A: Sarah Winnemucca Hopkins (1844–1891), daughter of the Paiute chief, Winnemucca, wrote this autobiographical book, which described the poor living conditions and treatment afforded to Nevada's native citizens. The book was one of the first ever written by an Native American.

Stewart Indian School

Q: What was the name of the Indian school established in Carson City that operated for nearly ninety years?

A: The Stewart Indian School opened on December 17, 1890, as the Clear Creek Indian Training Center. The name was later changed to the Carson Indian Training School, the Stewart Institute (after U.S. Senator William Stewart, who was instrumental in getting federal funds to establish the school), and, eventually, the Stewart Indian School. It closed in September 1980.

Fort Churchill

Q: What was the name of the bloody battle in May 1860 between white settlers and the Paiutes that resulted in the U.S. Army's decision to construct Fort Churchill?

A: The battle is generally called the Pyramid Lake Indian War of 1860. Following many indignities, including the kidnapping of two Indian women, a group of Indians retaliated by burning a trading post called Williams Station, located near present-day Lake Lahontan and killed three whites. In response, a citizen militia was formed in Virginia City that consisted of one hundred five ill-prepared, untrained volunteers. The force headed for the Indians' camp at Pyramid Lake but rode into a well-planned ambush. Seventy-six members of the militia were killed and most of the rest were wounded. The battle caused widespread hysteria among Nevada's white population. A second battle ensued in May 1860 and this time a more disciplined force of 549 volunteers and 207 regular army troops from California routed the Indians. In August 1860, the U.S. Government constructed Fort Churchill on the banks of the Carson River (between present-day Dayton and Fallon) to protect settlers from further hostilities.

Q: Where was the first Indian school opened in Nevada?

A: On March 1, 1878, a school was opened on the Pyramid Lake Paiute Reservation. It was enlarged to become a boarding school in 1882.

Q: When were Native American children allowed to attend public schools in Nevada?

A: Native American children were permitted to attend public schools in 1932 but it wasn't until 1956 that all Indian day schools became public schools.

Q: What mining town's name is derived from a Shoshone legend about a man-eating giant?

A: The name of Jarbidge, a northeastern Nevada town, comes from "Tswhawbitts," a mythical giant who the Shoshone people believed lived in the Jarbidge Canyon. The giant preyed on Indians, whom he tossed into a basket on his back.

Q: Who led the citizen militia that was soundly defeated during the first battle of the Pyramid Lake War?

A: Major William Ormsby, a pioneering Carson City businessman (he opened the first hotel in Carson City) led the militia into the ambush and died during the battle. The former Ormsby County (now part of the consolidated city-county of Carson City) was named for him.

Q: Who were the giant, redheaded Indians?

A: A legendary race of Northern Nevada Indians allegedly stood seven to nine feet tall and boasted bright red hair. The giants, who supposedly lived in Lovelock Cave near the Humboldt Sink, are part of Northern Paiute legend. Bones found in the cave in the 1930s were believed to prove their existence until they were remeasured in the late 1970s and found to be of normal size. The reddish hair, later tests showed, was the result of red ochre paint used in burial preparations by many Great Basin tribes.

Dat-so-la-lee
Photo courtesy of Nevada Historical Society

Q: What was the name of the famed Washoe basketmaker whose prized works are much sought after by collectors?

A: Dat-so-la-lee (circa 1835 to1925) would spend as much as a year working on a single basket. Her baskets are displayed in the Nevada State Museum and the Nevada Historical Society.

Q: What nut was an important staple in the diet of most Nevada tribes?

A: Pine nuts, found in the cones of the piñon pine tree, were prized because they could be stored and eaten during the winter, when other foods were more scarce.

Q: When did Nevada tribal members gain the right to vote?

A: All of America's aboriginal people, including Nevada's tribes, were granted the right to vote by the U.S. Congress in 1924.

Q: By what unflattering name did many emigrants and early western writers, including Mark Twain, call the Northern Paiutes and other Great Basin tribes?

A: The Paiutes and other Great Basin and California tribes were sometimes called "digger" Indians because the women often were seen digging with sticks for bulbs and roots.

Q: Where did General Patrick E. Conner attack a large encampment of northeastern Shoshone tribes, effectively ending Indian raids on travelers on the Emigrant Trail?

A: This event was the Bear River Massacre (also called the Battle of Bear River) in Idaho on January 29, 1863. Following the attack, the western Shoshones signed a formal non-aggression treaty on October 1, 1863.

Lost City Museum
Photo by Las Vegas News Bureau

Q: Where is the Lost City Museum?

A: Ninety miles northeast of Las Vegas in the town of Overton, the unique Lost City Museum highlights the culture and civilization of the Anasazi.

Q: Who was the Paiute war chief of the Pyramid Lake War?

A: Numaga, also called Young Winnemucca, finally agreed to lead the tribe after the burning of Williams Station.

Numaga
Photo courtesy of Nevada Historical Society

Q: Who was the "Paiute Messiah?"

A: Paiute shaman Wovoka (also called Jack Wilson), from Yerington, gained national attention in 1889 with his "Ghost Dance" movement, which predicted the disappearance of the white man and a return to earlier times. The movement was embraced by tribes throughout the country, particularly the Plains Indians, and was partially responsible for misunderstandings that resulted in the Battle at Wounded Knee, the last major Indian battle in the U.S. The movement died out after 1891.

Q: What name is given by archaeologists to the native people who inhabited the Pyramid Lake basin from about 1800 B.C to 1844 B.C.?

A: These people are said to be part of the Lovelock Culture, named because of related artifacts found in the Lovelock Cave.

Q: When and where was the last Indian skirmish in the United States?

A: On February 26, 1911, a small band of roaming Shoshone men, women and children, led by "Shoshone Mike," were cornered in a shoot-out north of Winnemucca. The group, later described as the last free Indians in the country, had allegedly killed four stockmen in January. State police and a sheriff's posse killed the men and arrested the others, who were later sent to out-of-state reservations.

COWBOYS AND COWTOWNS
From Ranchers to Rodeos

❖❖❖❖❖❖❖❖❖❖❖❖❖❖❖❖❖❖❖❖❖❖

Q: What famous outlaw gang is believed to have robbed the First National Bank in Winnemucca in September 1900?

A: Butch Cassidy's Hole in the Wall Gang, apparently operating without Butch Cassidy or the Sundance Kid, is believed to be behind the bank robbery. The gang took $32,000 and no one was ever arrested.

Q: What Englishman established the first permanent ranch at Big Meadows in northeastern Nevada?

A: George Lovelock settled in the region and started the first ranching operation in the area. In the late 1860s, Lovelock donated a right-of-way to the Central Pacific Railroad and a town site, which became Lovelock.

Q: The descendants of what presidents still own a ranch near Genoa?

A: Descendants of John Quincy Adams the second president, and Quincy Adams, the sixth president, still own the Adams House, a 1,500-acre ranch near Genoa. The two-story colonial brick home was built in 1856 by Rufus and John Quincy Adams V.

Q: What famed crooner once owned a large ranch near Elko and was named honorary mayor of Elko?

A: Singer Bing Crosby owned a large ranch at North Fork, about forty miles north of Elko.

Q: What was the name of the ranch near Las Vegas that was the home of 1920s and 1930s cowboy movie star Rex Bell and actress Clara Bow?

A: Bell and Bow, who married in Las Vegas in 1931, owned the Walking Box Ranch, sixty miles south of Las Vegas.

Q: What Nevada governor was originally a cattle baron, who introduced the first full-blooded Hereford and Durham cattle to Nevada?

A: In the late nineteenth century, John "Honest John" Sparks co-owned huge tracts of land in northern Elko County and southern Idaho, where he had more than 70,000 head of cattle. In 1902, he was elected Governor of Nevada, serving until his death in office in 1908.

Governor John Sparks

Q: Who brought the first cattle into Nevada?

A: Colonel John Reese, sent to Nevada in 1851 by Mormon leader Brigham Young to establish a colony, brought into the state the first livestock for beef and dairy production. He founded the first permanent settlement in Genoa, which he called Mormon Station.

Q: What catastrophic event occurred in 1889 to 1890 that nearly destroyed Nevada's livestock industry?

A: During the "White Winter" of 1889 to 1890, nearly one hundred inches of snow fell—the heaviest recorded snowfall in northern Nevada history. An estimated ninety to ninety-five percent of the state's livestock died during that winter.

Q: What hotel magnate owns a huge ranching operation that stretches along twenty-nine miles of the East Walker River?

A: Barron Hilton, chairman of Hilton Hotels, owns the 480,000-acre Flying M Ranch, about twenty-five miles south of Yerington.

Q: What famed western artist-writer was once arrested in Nevada for cattle rustling and spent time in the Nevada State Prison?

A: Western writer Will James was convicted of cattle rustling near Ely in 1914 and served a year in the state prison.

Q: In what community is the annual Western Art Roundup?

A: This event, which attracts dozens of western artists, is held in Winnemucca.

Q: What rural Nevada museum boasts a reconstructed Pony Express Station?

A: The fine Northeastern Nevada Museum in Elko is home of the former Ruby Valley Pony Express Station, built in 1860. The station, made of rough logs and wood planks, was used between April 1860 and October 1861 and was originally located sixty miles south of Elko in the Ruby Valley.

Q: What is the name of the highway that begins in Winnemucca and ends at Crescent City, California?

A: This route is called the Winnemucca to the Sea Highway. It was originally proposed in the 1920s by "Fritz" Buckingham, a local rancher, who felt there was a need for a shortcut from northern Nevada to the Pacific Northwest. Buckingham served many years in the Nevada legislature and pursued his dream, which was finally completed in 1962. A large redwood log that washed onto the beach at Crescent City was later transported to Winnemucca to commemorate the road.

"Winnemucca to the Sea Highway"

Q: Where is the Buckaroo Hall of Fame?

A: This nice, small museum of western art, memorabilia and historic photographs is housed in Winnemucca.

Q: What famed saddlemaker shop is located in Elko?

A: The G. S. Garcia Saddlemaker Shop, part of the J. M. Capriola's Western Wear Store in Elko, has been making hand-tooled leather saddles since 1896. The shop was started by Mexican artisan Guadalupe S. Garcia, who died in 1937. His son, Les, has carried on the family tradition.

Q: What Nevada cowboy poet has appeared several times on the *Tonight Show*?

A: Bruce "Waddie" Mitchell of Elko, who has published several books of cowboy poetry, appeared three times on the *Tonight Show* in the 1980s. In 1987, he was given the Governor's Award in the Arts.

Q: Where is the home of the Western Folklife Center?

A: This organization, dedicated to preserving western art and culture, is headquartered in Elko. The Western Folklife Center is the sponsor of the Cowboy Poetry Gathering in January and the Cowboy Music Gathering in June.

Bruce "Waddie" Mitchell

Q: Where is the annual Cowboy Poetry Gathering?

A: Elko, which traveler writer Lowell Thomas once called, "the last true cowtown in America," is home of this event.

Cowboy singer, Gary McMahon, at the Cowboy Poetry Gathering

Cowboy landing hard at Reno Rodeo
Photo by Reno News Bureau

Q: When was the Reno Rodeo started?

A: The first Reno Rodeo, originally called the "Nevada Round-Up," was held in 1919. It has been held annually except for several breaks in the 1920s and in the early 1930s. Western artist Will James produced artwork for the first Reno Rodeo program, which was his first professional art sale.

Q: What city is host to the annual National Finals Rodeo?

A: Las Vegas is home of this grand event, which attracts the top rodeo cowboys each year.

Q: What is the oldest continuous rodeo in Nevada?

A: The oldest continuous rodeo is the Winnemucca Rodeo, which has been held since 1921.

Q: What infamous Nevada gunman, who later made a fortune in mining, narrowly avoided the hangman's noose for killing two sheepherders—even after the real murderers had confessed?

A: This colorful figure was Jackson Lee Davis, known as "Diamondfield" Jack Davis. In 1895, Davis was hired by cattlemen to intimidate Idaho sheepherders. He was falsely accused, then convicted of killing two Mormon sheepherders and sentenced to hang. Despite his appeals and confessions by the real killers, he languished in prison until 1902, when he was finally pardoned. A few years later, he struck it rich in Goldfield, then drifted into obscurity. He died in Las Vegas in 1949 after being struck by a car.

Q: What agricultural community is the oldest town in eastern Nevada?

A: The farming town of Panaca is the oldest, founded by Mormon settlers in 1864. While the presence of silver—the name Panaca derives from the Paiute word for silver—first attracted the Mormons to the area, the town's longevity is due to its farming. In the 1870s, Panaca produced much of the wood and food for the nearby mining boomtown of Pioche.

Q: What Battle Mountain cowboy was the Professional Rodeo Cowboy Association World Champion in 1978?

A: Joe Marvel, who was considered one of the rodeo circuit's most stylish saddle bronco riders.

Spring Mountain Ranch

Q: What ranch near Las Vegas, now a state park, has been owned by Chester Lauck (of "Lum and Abner" fame), Vera Krupp (wife of German munitions manufacturer Alfried Krupp) and Howard Hughes?

A: This celebrity hideaway, located fifteen miles west of Las Vegas, at the base of the magnificent Wilson Cliffs, is Spring Mountain Ranch. The 520-acre ranch became a state park in 1974.

Q: Who was the first woman to be designated Nevada's "Cattleman of the Year?"

A: Louise Marvel, daughter of W. T. Jenkins, who started the first major ranching outfit in Battle Mountain in 1873, was given this honor in 1962. For a time her ranch was the largest in northern Nevada, spreading over parts of five counties.

Q: What two Hollywood actors, who appeared in a few westerns, purchased ranches in the Elko area in the late 1940s?

A: Actors Jimmy Stewart and Joel McCrae bought spreads in the area following Bing Crosby's purchase of land north of Elko. Stewart owned the Wine Cup Ranch, thirty miles north of Wells, while McCrae owned a place in the Ruby Valley.

Q: What famed Las Vegas singer is also a top Arabian horse breeder?

A: Wayne Newton raises championship Arabians.

NATURAL NEVADA
Landscape of Grandeur

❖❖❖❖❖❖❖❖❖❖❖❖❖❖❖❖❖❖❖❖❖

Q: Who named the Great Basin region?

A: Explorer John C. Fremont coined the name Great Basin for the area between Utah's Wasatch Range and the Sierra Nevada Range. He incorrectly described the region as one large basin, when, in fact, it is about seventy-five basins separated by mountain ranges running north to south.

Q: What unique characteristic is shared by all rivers in the Great Basin?

A: Rivers in the Great Basin do not flow to an ocean, like most other rivers. Instead, the rivers flow inland, either to a lake or into a large sink.

Q: What is the only Nevada lake with an outlet to the sea?

A: Man-made Lake Mead, created from the Colorado River, flows into the Gulf of California.

Q: What was the name of the huge prehistoric inland sea believed to have once covered much of western Nevada?

A: Geologists believe an ancient ocean, called Lake Lahontan, covered about 8,450 square miles. It was to have extended 250 miles from the Nevada-Oregon border to modern day Hawthorne, Nevada, 132 miles south of Reno. Most of Lake Lahontan dried up about 15,000 years ago, leaving behind several smaller lakes, including Pyramid and Walker Lakes.

Q: About how much water evaporates annually from Lake Mead?

A: Approximately 600,000 acre-feet of water is absorbed into the air each year at Lake Mead.

Q: True or false. The single leaf piñon pine does not grow north of the Humboldt River in Nevada.

A: True. The single leaf piñon is not found north of the river. Botanists believe this is either because of some unknown condition that makes the area unfriendly to piñons or simply because its seeds have not yet been dispersed in that area by birds.

Q: What trees found primarily in the Sierra Nevada Range are the world's largest variety of pine?

A: The sugar pine is the largest pine, growing to more than two hundred feet in height and six feet in diameter. The sugar pine also boasts the longest pine cones of any variety, as much as two feet long.

Q: What is the name of the 600-foot high sand dune found east of Fallon?

A: This mound, a remnant of ancient Lake Lahontan, is named Sand Mountain or "Singing" Sand Mountain, because of the sound the wind makes when it blows across the dunes.

Q: How many antelope are estimated to be living in Nevada?

A: About 18,500 antelope are thought to be roaming the state, mostly in northern Nevada.

Q: Where does Nevada rank nationally in development and use of geothermal resources for energy production?

A: The state ranks second after California in geothermal power production. As of 2003, it had fourteen plants at ten locations producing approximately 1.64 million megawatt hours of electricity, enough to power 80,000 typical homes.

Sand Mountain, near Fallon
Photo courtesy of Nevada Department of Transportation

Q: What percentage of Nevada is forest land?

A: Forests cover some 8.6 million acres, but Nevada is so large that it only represents twelve percent.

Q: What part of the Great Basin in Nevada is the richest in terms of number of tree species?

A: The east slope of the Sierra Nevada is the most tree-rich area with Utah juniper, single leaf piñon, curl leaf mountain mahogany, black cottonwood, ponderosa, Jeffrey and Washoe Pines, white and red firs, western juniper, mountain hemlock, and western white, lodgepole and whitebark pines.

Q: What is the lowest major elevational vegetation zone found in Nevada?

A: The Shadscale Zone is the lowest. Named for its dominant plant, the shadscale, it is the zone found at the bottom of low, saline intermontane valleys (usually between 4,600 and 5,000 feet in elevation). No trees can grow in this zone, which is considered desert.

Q: True or false, Nevada is the driest state in the nation.

A: True. The statewide average annual precipitation is a mere nine inches.

Q: What is the largest natural lake located entirely within Nevada?

A: Pyramid Lake, located thirty-five miles north of Reno, is twenty-seven miles long and nine miles wide.

Q: What island in Pyramid Lake contains North America's largest nesting colony of white pelicans?

A: Anaho Island, at the south end of the lake, is home of an estimated 7,500 white pelicans, the largest nesting colony in North America. The island is also the nesting grounds for cormorants and California gulls.

Q: What is the pyramid in Pyramid Lake made of?

A: The namesake pyramid-shaped rock in Pyramid Lake is made of tufa, a rocklike material formed when calcium-bearing fresh water bubbles up into alkaline lake water rich with carbonates. The resulting limestone deposits grow—as long as they remain submerged—into a variety of shapes, such as the lake's pyramid.

Q: What endangered prehistoric fish species can still be found in Pyramid Lake?

A: The cui ui. This tiny sucker fish can live to be forty years old and has long been an important part of the Pyramid Lake Paiute tribal traditions and culture.

Q: What Nevada community is second only to Laredo, Texas, for having the most record-high temperatures in the U.S.?

A: Laughlin, at the state's southernmost tip, is Nevada's hottest spot and the nation's second hottest. The highest recorded temperature in Laughlin–also the state record highest temperature–is 125º F, which was recorded on June 29, 1994.

Pyramid Lake

Q: What is the lowest recorded temperature in Nevada?

A: The lowest temperature was -50º F, recorded at San Jacinto (about twenty miles south of Jackpot) on January 8, 1937.

Q: Where in Nevada was the world's largest cutthroat trout caught?

A: The world record for a cutthroat trout was set in December 1925 by John Skimmerhorn, a Paiute Indian, who caught a forty-one-pound Lahontan cutthroat trout in Pyramid Lake.

Q: What bird acts as the primary seed disperser of the limber pine and whitebark pine?

A: The Clark's nutcracker not only consumes the pine seeds, but also caches them underground. If unretrieved, the seeds germinate and become trees. This process is the only natural way these pines proliferate.

Q: Where is the place of lowest elevation in Nevada?

A: The lowest place is 470 feet above sea level on the Colorado River, just south of Laughlin.

Q: What is the name of the popular annual event conducted in the Black Rock Desert, north of Reno, that celebrates radical self-expression and self-reliance?

A: This unusual counterculture event is called Burning Man and it has been held in Nevada's Black Rock Desert since 1990. In 2003, more than 30,000 people attended Burning Man, which is usually held during the week prior to and including Labor Day. The anything-goes event, which encourages artistic self-expression, culminates in the burning of a 30 to 60-foot wooden representation of a man (the Burning Man).

Q: What is the world's oldest living species of tree, which can be found in Nevada?

Bristlecone Pine

A: The bristlecone pine found in the Great Basin National Park and a handful of other mountain ranges, can live to be more than 4,000 years old.

Q: What is the rarest pine tree variety found in Nevada?

A: The Washoe pine is the rarest pine in Nevada and the second rarest in North America (after the reclusive Torrey pine). The Washoe pine is only found in a few mountains in western Nevada and northeastern California. The largest known grove is on Mount Rose, Nevada, at the head of Galena Creek.

Q: True of False: Reno, Nevada is west of Los Angeles, California?

A: True: If you look at a map, Reno is actually slightly west of Los Angeles because of the shape of California's coast line.

Q: What variety of tree, found in Nevada, has the greatest elevational range of any tree in North America, growing everywhere from sea level to 12,000 feet?

A: The Lodgepole pine is the most widespread of western pines, extending from coastal southeast Alaska to Baja, California, to the Black Hills of South Dakota. It can grow in nearly every climate and elevation. In Nevada, it is found in the Sierra, Virginia and Sweetwater Ranges.

Q: Where can you find the rare swamp cedar grove in Nevada?

A: This grove of trees, which are actually Rocky Mountain junipers, can be found in a wet valley bottom in the middle of Spring Valley, located between the Snake and Schell Creek ranges in eastern Nevada. They are called swamp cedars because of their reddish color and are considered an unusual ecotype because they have adapted to grow in thickets in a highly saline soil, completely absent of other trees. Some live to be more than 300 years old.

Q: What trees, found in Nevada, are often called "quakies."

A: The beautiful quaking aspens are sometimes called "quakies" because their round, silver dollar-sized leaves tremble in the slightest wind.

Q: What is the only species of birch tree found in Nevada?

A: The water birch is the only type of birch indigenous to the state. It is found along streams in some east-central Nevada valleys, usually between 5,000 and 8,000 feet in elevation.

Q: What family of shrubs, found in Nevada and Utah, produce a beverage sometimes called "Mormon tea?"

A: The Ephedras, broomlike shrubs that can grow up to three feet tall, can be used to make a medicinal tea that has been called "Mormon tea," "Settler's tea," and "Squaw tea."

Q: What shrub did writer Mark Twain say made "a very fair fuel, but as a vegetable it is a distinguished failure?"

A: This lowly shrub was the sagebrush. Twain wrote his remarks about the state's most ubiquitous shrub in his classic, *Roughing It*, which described his years in Nevada.

Q: What appropriately named shrub is a valuable food source for range cattle during the winter?

A: Winterfat gets its name from the fact it is an important wintertime browsing food for domestic livestock as well as elk and deer. A member of the goosefoot family of shrubs, it is an important source of protein and vitamin A for animals.

Q: What heavenly lake is high in the East Humboldt Range?

A: Beautiful Angel Lake, elevation 8,378 feet, is located twelve miles south of Wells.

Q: What shrub, usually found on Nevada's alkali flats, was described as the "infernal prickly yarb" by nineteenth-century newspaperman Dan De Quille?

A: Greasewood thrives in dense alkaline or saline soils. Despite De Quille's depiction, greasewood is considered a decent forage for livestock.

Q: What is the longest river in Nevada?

A: Wandering across northern Nevada for some 500 miles, the Humboldt River stretches from north of Wells to the Humboldt Sink, southwest of Lovelock.

Q: What is the only type of trout native to western Nevada?

A: The Lahontan cutthroat trout is the only trout indigenous to the western part of the state. It is found mainly in Pyramid, Walker and Topaz Lakes.

Q: What is Nevada's only deep-water fish?

A: The Mackinaw trout, introduced into Lake Tahoe in 1885, is the state's only deep-water fish.

Q: What is the most common big game animal found in Nevada?

A: The mule deer is the most common big game animal in the state. There are an estimated 200,000 spread throughout Nevada. The most common animal in the state is the black-tailed jackrabbit.

Q: Approximately how many species of birds can be found in Nevada?

A: Since birds are so migratory, the best approximation is that there are more than three hundred seventy species of birds in the state. Additionally, there are an estimated one hundred twenty-nine species of mammals and sixty-four types of reptile and amphibian species.

Q: What is the tallest peak in the Ruby Mountains?

A: The Rubies are one of fourteen designated wilderness areas in Nevada. Ruby Dome is 11,387 feet.

Q: Where in Nevada can you find a large colony of white-faced ibises?

A: One of the three largest colonies in the U.S. of white-faced ibises can be found at Carson Lake, a shallow lake located ten miles south of Fallon. An estimated 4,000 pairs of ibises nest at the lake.

Q: Where is the steepest vertical rise in Nevada?

A: In the Spring Mountains of southern Nevada, you can climb from an elevation of 2,000 feet at the base of the range to 11,918 feet, at the summit of Charleston Peak.

Q: How many acres of reservoirs are in Nevada?

A: Nevada is home to more than 44,000 acres of man-made reservoirs.

Q: How many kinds of rattlesnakes are found in Nevada?

A: There are seven different types of rattlers, all found in the southern part of the state. They are: the south-western speckled, the Panamint, the western diamond-back, the Mohave rattler, the sidewinder, the Great Basin rattlesnake and the mountain king snake.

Q: What is the highest spot in southern Nevada (Clark County)?

A: Charleston Peak in the Spring Mountains rises to 11,918 feet.

Q: Where is the only glacier in Nevada?

A: The cirque at the base of Wheeler Peak, in Great Basin National Park, is the location of the only glacial remnant in the state.

Q: How many miles of streams can be found in Nevada?

A: There are 2,760 miles of streams.

Q: Where is Nevada's largest concentration of wintering bald eagles?

A: These majestic birds can be found at the Lahontan State Recreation Area, located eighteen miles east of Fallon. The eagles roost and hunt from shoreline trees at the Lahontan Reservoir because of the large fishery.

Q: What shrub, found throughout Nevada, is considered the most abundant shrub in North America?

A: Big sagebrush can be found all over the West. Its natural range is from western Nebraska to Montana and British Columbia to New Mexico and lower California.

Q: In which county will you find the greatest concentration of state parks?

A: Lincoln County in eastern Nevada has five state parks.

Q: How many state parks are in Nevada?

A: Twenty-two.

Elephant Rock, pictured here, is one of the many unique sandstone formations found at the Valley of Fire State Park in southern Nevada.

Q: What was Nevada's first state park?

A: Valley of Fire State Park, located about an hour northeast of Las Vegas, was created in 1923. At 34,880 acres, it is the largest state park and noted for its unusual, fiery red sandstone formations.

Q: What is the smallest state park?

A: The Belmont Courthouse, a historic two-story brick building built in 1876, was designated a state park in 1974. The site measures one and six-tenths acres and is located in the ghost town of Belmont, forty-five miles north of Tonopah.

Stella Lake, Great Basin National Park

Q: How many national parks can be found in Nevada?

A: Two: Great Basin National Park and Death Valley National Park. Great Basin National Park is located seventy miles southeast of Ely, in east-central Nevada and was created in 1986 to commemorate the unique geology, history, plant and animal life found in the Great Basin region. Death Valley National Park, which straddles the California-Nevada border about a hundred miles northwest of Las Vegas, was created in 1994.

Q: What percentage of Nevada is covered by sagebrush?

A: Approximately 40% of Nevada is covered with this shrub.

Q: By what popular name is the irritating Russian thistle, found throughout Nevada, known?

A: This pesky plant is also known as tumbleweed.

Joshua Tree in Nevada

Q: What wildlife refuge is home to twenty-six species of plants and animals found nowhere else in the world?

A: The Ash Meadows National Wildlife Refuge twenty-five miles northwest of Pahrump, is a unique habitat. Rare species at the reserve include four endangered fish: the Ash Meadows speckled dace, the Ash Meadows Amargosa pupfish, the Warm Springs pupfish and the Devil's Hole pupfish.

Q: What desert tree was named by Mormon pioneers because they imagined its limbs were arms pointing the way to the Promised Land?

A: The unusual Joshua tree, found in the southern part of Nevada, is the largest species of the yucca genus and can grow to thirty feet tall. It is also called yucca palm.

Q: What is the only poisonous reptile found in Nevada?

A: The banded Gila monster, found in southern Nevada, is the only poisonous lizard in the state. It is considered extremely rare and is an endangered species.

Q: What is the most common lizard in Nevada?

A: The western fence lizard, found throughout the state is the most common. It is brown with a bright blue stomach. The most common snake is the Great Basin gopher snake.

Q: What is Nevada's largest raptor?

A: Biologists believe there may be nearly 1,200 nesting pairs of the golden eagle, mostly concentrated in the northern portion of the state.

Q: In what mountain range is 13,063-foot Wheeler Peak?

A: The Snake Range in eastern Nevada. Wheeler Peak is the second tallest point in Nevada within the Great Basin National Park.

Q: Where can you pick the hearts of gold cantaloupe?

A: The agricultural community of Fallon is home base for this tasty melon, which is feted there each fall during the Hearts of Gold Cantaloupe Festival.

Q: What name is given to the furious westerly winds that blow down the eastern Sierra ranges of western Nevada?

A: These mighty gusts, which Mark Twain described as "a peculiarly scriptural wind, in that no man knoweth 'whence it cometh'," are called zephyrs, or more specifically, Washoe zephyrs.

Q: What percentage of Nevada is under cultivation?

A: Only one and fourth-tenths percent of Nevada is under cultivation. The production is mostly in hay and forage crops.

Q: Who once called Lake Tahoe, "the fairest picture the whole earth affords?"

A: Writer Mark Twain (Samuel Clemens) scribed those words in his classic book, *Roughing It*, which traces his years in Nevada and California in the 1860s.

Q: What is the average depth of Lake Tahoe?

A: This beautiful alpine lake on the California-Nevada border has an average depth of 1,000 feet. It is 1,645 feet at its deepest point, making it the tenth deepest lake in the world and third deepest in North America. Lake Tahoe contains an estimated 122-million acre feet of water—enough to cover the entire state of California to a depth of fourteen inches.

Q: What state has the largest number of wild horses?

A: The state of Nevada is home to an estimated 28,000 wild horses, or seventy percent of the wild horses believed to be roaming free in the U.S.

Q: Where is the largest wildlife refuge in the lower 48 states?

A: The Desert Wildlife Refuge stretches over some 1.5 million acres in southern Nevada, including the Desert, Las Vegas, Pintwater and Sheep Ranges. The refuge is home to more bighorn sheep (an estimated 1,500) than any other place in the world.

Q: What shrub's supple green branches are woven into baskets by a number of Great Basin region tribes?

A: The coyote willow, which can grow to six feet tall, is used to make baskets. The willows are found along streams and irrigation ditches in Nevada.

Q: What obnoxious, itchy shrub can be found only in one place in Nevada?

A: Fortunately, poison oak, common in California's coastal ranges and on the western side of the Sierra Nevadas, has only been found in a canyon near Pyramid Lake.

Lake Tahoe

Devil's Hole, home of the Devil's Hole pupfish

Q: What tiny fish was once found only in three springs in the Pahrump Valley?

A: Two of three of the original subspecies of the Pahrump killifish are extinct. The third survives only because it was transplanted in the Shoshone Pond near Ely and in Corn Creek Springs.

Q: Where is Devil's Hole and who lives there?

A: Devil's Hole is in the Ash Meadows Wildlife Refuge and is part of Death Valley National Park. Located in southwestern Nevada, Devil's Hole is home for the Devil's Hole pupfish, a species only found in this deep crack in the earth.

Q: What are the names of the two major deserts found in Nevada?

A: The Mojave and the Great Basin Deserts. The demarcation line between the two deserts is located roughly 175 miles north of Las Vegas. Their most obvious physical difference is the large, spiky Joshua trees which thrive in the warmer Mojave but not generally in the high desert country of the Great Basin. Travelers first encounter joshuas while driving south of Tonopah on U.S. Highway 95 or south of Caliente on U.S. Highway 93.

Q: What fish is only found in the warm springs and creeks of Soldier Meadows in the Black Rock Desert?

A: The tiny desert dace is this extremely rare fish.

Q: When was Nevada's first state-owned fish hatchery built?

A: The state's first hatchery facility was built in 1885 in Carson City at a cost of $500. Prior to its opening, there had been small, private hatcheries.

Q: How many pounds of fish are produced each year by Nevada's fish hatcheries?

A: The state's five hatcheries produce 230,000 pounds of fish per year, mostly kokanee salmon and rainbow, brown, lake and cutthroat trout.

Q: What endangered fish is only found in eastern Nevada?

A: The Pahranagat roundtail chub is only found in the outflow of Ash Springs in eastern Nevada. Fewer than forty are believed to exist.

Q: What fish, found throughout Nevada, is an essential food for the cutthroat trout and the bird populations of Pyramid Lake?

A: The tui chub is the food base for both the Lahontan cutthroat trout and the nesting birds on Anaho Island.

Q: Yes or no, does Nevada contain more mountain ranges than any other state?

A: Yes. Despite the popular perception that the state is a dry, flat desert landscape, it has more identified mountain ranges than any other state.

Q: How many mountain ranges are estimated to be in Nevada?

A: Depending on the source, there are one hundred sixty ranges (historian Russell Elliott), two hundred fifty ranges (author Deke Castleman) or three hundred fourteen ranges (author and naturalist Alvin McLane). Nearly all run in a northeast-southwest direction and, according to McLane, not all have been named.

Q: How many Nevada mountain peaks measure more than 12,000 feet high?

A: Five: Boundary Peak (13,140), Wheeler Peak (13,063), Jeff Davis (12,771), Mount Baker (12,298) and Mount Moriah (12,067).

Q: How many mountain ranges in Nevada have one or more peaks exceeding 11,000 feet?

A: Nine: Grant Range, Schell Creek Range, Snake Range, Spring Mountains, Toiyabe Range, Toquima Range, Wassuk Mountains, White Mountains and White Pine Range.

Q: Where can you find the "Seven Sisters," "Elephant Rock" and "Mouse's Tank?"

A: These colorful monikers refer to unique formations found in the Valley of Fire State Park.

Q: What natural phenomenon did an eastern Nevada farmer stumble onto in the 1880s?

A: In the early 1880s, Absalom Lehman found a huge series of limestone caves filled with magnificent formations. The discovery became the Lehman Caves National Monument in 1922, then part of the Great Basin National Park in 1986.

Elephant Rock
Photo by Las Vegas News Bureau

SCOUNDRELS AND STATESMEN
Politics in the Silver State

❖❖❖❖❖❖❖❖❖❖❖❖❖❖❖❖❖❖❖❖

Q: Who was Nevada's only territorial governor?

A: James Warren Nye was appointed territorial governor in 1861 and served until 1864. Interestingly, Nye, who was born in New York, left his family in his home state during his entire term as governor.

Q: Who was the first native Nevadan to serve as governor of Nevada?

A: Emmet Derby Boyle, who served from 1915 to 1922, was born on July 26, 1879 in Gold Hill, near Virginia City.

Q: Who were the first native Nevadans to serve in the Nevada state legislature?

A: Frank P. Langan, born in American Flat in 1865, and George D. Pyne, born in Virginia City in 1866, were both elected to the Nevada state assembly in 1889.

Q: Who was Nevada's first elected governor?

A: Henry Goode Blasdel was Nevada's first elected governor, serving from 1864 to 1870. Blasdel was born on January 29, 1825 near Lawrenceburg, Indiana, and moved to Nevada in 1861. He died in his home in Oakland, California, in 1900.

Q: Who was the first Nevada governor to die in office?

A: Charles Clark Stevenson, Nevada's fifth governor, died near the end of his first term, on September 21, 1890. He was succeeded by Lieutenant Governor Frank Bell.

Q: Who was the only governor to die in the Governor's Mansion?

A: Frederick Bennett Balzar, who served from 1927 to 1934, died in the mansion on March 21, 1934.

Governor Henry G. Blasdel
Photo courtesy of Nevada Historical Society

Q: How many native Nevadans have served as governor?

A: Seven: Emmet Boyle (1915 to 1922); Frederick Balzar (1927 to 1934); Morley Griswold (1934); Richard Kirman (1935 to 1938); Edward Carville (1939 to 1945); Charles Russell (1951 to 1958); and Paul Laxalt,(1967 to 1970).

Q: Who was the first governor to occupy the Governor's Mansion?

A: Acting Governor Denver S. Dickerson and his wife moved into the mansion in July 1909, and lived there for about a year. Mrs. Una (Reilly) Dickerson was born in the mining town of Hamilton, Nevada. Their daughter, June, is the only child to have been born in the mansion (on September 2, 1909).

Q: Since Nevada became a state in 1864, has the state had more Democratic governors or more Republican governors?

A: Republican, by one. Of Nevada's twenty-seven elected governors, including lieutenant governors elevated to the job, twelve have been Republicans, eleven have been Democrats, and four were from the short-lived Silver or Silver-Democrat Party.

Q: How many Nevada governors were foreign-born?

A: Three: Frank Bell (1890), who was born in Toronto, Canada; John Edward Jones (1895–1896), who was born in Montgomeryshire, Wales; and Reinhold Sadler (1896–1902), who was born in Czarnikau, Posen Province, Prussia.

Q: Who were Nevada's first two United States Senators?

A: Republicans James Nye, formerly the territorial governor, joined William Stewart as Nevada's representatives in the U.S. Senate on December 15, 1864. Nye remained in the Senate until 1873, while Stewart served until 1875, then again from 1887 to 1905.

Q: Who was Nevada's first Congressman?

A: H. G. Worthington was elected as the state's first member of the U.S. House of Representatives. He served from 1864 to 1865.

Governor Frank Bell
Photo courtesy of Nevada Historical Society

Q: What unusual duty was assigned to Nevada's lieutenant governors elected between 1865 and 1873?

A: During those years, the lieutenant governor was ex officio warden of the state prison. The duty could be hazardous—in 1871, Lieutenant Governor Frank Denver and four guards were wounded during a prison breakout. The law was finally changed by the state legislature after Denver was accused of mismanagement.

Q: What unique method is used in Nevada to break an election tie vote?

A: Under Nevada state law, a deadlocked election is decided by drawing lots. Traditionally, this has been done by tossing a coin, drawing straws, or deciding the race with a game of high card. In November 2004, Robert Swetich and Raymond Urrizaga each received 1,847 votes for a seat on the White Pine County Commission. The election was decided when both candidates agreed to a game of high card (each man draws one card; high card wins). Urrizaga won by drawing a Queen of Clubs while Swetich drew a seven of diamonds.

Q: What current member of Britain's House of Lords was born in Reno, Nevada?

A: The Nevada-born Lord is Garret Wellesley, the "Earl Cowley," with courtesy titles that include Baron Cowley of Somerset and Viscount Dangan. Wellesley's father, Christian Arthur Wellesley, moved to Nevada in the 1930s to obtain a divorce (not available at the time in England). The senior Lord Wellesley enjoyed northern Nevada and, after obtaining his divorce, built an 18th century-style English estate at the south end of Washoe Valley. He remarried to a Reno woman, Mary Elsie May, and they had two children, both born in Reno, Garret and a younger brother, Tim. In the mid-1970s, Garret Wellesley, then living in San Francisco, inherited his father's title, which included the family seat in Britain's House of Lords, and relocated to England.

Q: Who served the longest tenure as Nevada's representative in Congress?

A: Democrat Walter Baring, who served from 1949 to 1952, then from 1957 to 1972, served twenty years in the House of Representatives, twice as long as any other person has served as Nevada's Congressman.

Q: Who was the youngest person ever to serve in the Nevada state legislature?

A: Richard Kirman was elected to the state assembly in 1899 at the age of twenty-one. He later served as governor from 1935 to 1938.

Q: Who was the first woman elected to the Nevada legislature?

A: Sadie D. Hurst, a Republican from Reno, was the first woman legislator. She was elected to the state assembly in 1919 and served one term.

Q: Who was the first woman mayor in Nevada?

A: Dorothy Porter, a former Ziegfeld dancer, was the first woman in Nevada elected to a major city council, in 1953, then was elected mayor of North Las Vegas by her fellow council members the following year.

Q: Who was the first woman elected mayor of Las Vegas?

A: In 1990, Jan Laverty Jones was elected the first female mayor of the state's largest city.

Q: Who was the first woman elected to represent Nevada in the U.S. Congress?

A: Republican Barbara Vucanovich was elected to the Nevada District two seat in the U.S. House of Representatives in 1982 and reelected in every election through 1992.

Lieutenant Governor Sue Wagner

Q: Who was the first woman elected to statewide constitutional office?

A: Republican Patricia Cafferata, who was state treasurer from 1982 to 1986. In 1986, Democrat Frankie Sue Del Papa became the first female secretary of state. In 1990, three women were elected to statewide offices for the first time: Lieutenant Governor Sue Wagner (Republican) (pictured); Attorney General Frankie Sue Del Papa (Democrat); and Secretary of State Cheryl Lau (Republican).

Q: What two Nevada governors were not married during their terms?

A: Lewis Rice Bradley, the second governor (1871 to 1878), was a widower and Tasker L. Oddie, the twelfth governor (1911 to 1914), was not married during his term.

Governor Tasker L. Oddie
Photo courtesy of Nevada Historical Society

Q: When did women gain the right to vote in Nevada?

A: On November 3, 1914, Nevada voters approved a measure granting women the right to vote.

Q: Who was the first woman elected mayor of Reno?

A: In 1979, Barbara Bennett was elected the first female mayor of Reno. She resigned in 1983 to accept a state job.

Q: Who was the first woman elected to statewide office in Nevada?

A: Republican Edna C. Baker (1876-1957) was elected a University of Nevada system regent in 1916 and served until 1918.

Q: In what Nevada ranching community did a Nevada governor, a U.S. Congressman and a U.S. Senator all grow up on the same block?

A: This political neighborhood was in Lovelock. As children, Governor Charles Russell (1951 to 1958), Congressman Cliff Young (1953 to 1956), and Senator Alan Bible (1954 to 1974) all lived within a few houses of each other.

Q: What U.S. Senator from Nevada was sometimes called the "First Friend" by the media during the term of President Ronald Reagan?

A: Senator Paul Laxalt, who served from 1974 to 1986, was frequently called the "First Friend" because of his close personal relationship with President Reagan. The two had become friends when Reagan had been California's governor and Laxalt was Nevada's governor in the late 1960s.

Q: Who was the first Chinese-American elected to statewide office?

A: Lilly Fong of Las Vegas was elected to the University of Nevada Board of Regents in 1976 and served two terms.

Q: Who was the first African-American elected to the Nevada legislature?

A: Woodrow Wilson of Las Vegas was elected in 1966 to the state assembly as a Republican.

Q: Does Nevada have more registered voters who are Republicans or Democrats?

A: In 2004, 40.13 percent of the state's registered voters were Democrats while 40.54 percent were Republicans.

Q: In which presidential election did a majority of Nevadans not support either the Republican or Democratic party candidates?

A: In 1892, a majority of Nevadans supported the Silver Party candidates over the candidates of the two major parties. The Silver Party was a populist party of the late nineteenth century that attracted considerable support in Nevada because it espoused using silver (which Nevada produced in great quantity) as well as gold as the standard for national currency.

Q: What percentage of Nevada's population is registered to vote?

A: Only fifty-seven percent of those eligible to vote in the state are registered.

Q: When did Nevada adopt the principal of "one-man, one-vote," which determined that legislative districts should be apportioned by population rather than geography?

A: In 1965, the state was ordered by the federal court to apportion legislative districts by population. The move effectively ended decades of rural control.

Q: Who was the first woman to serve on the state supreme court?

A: Miriam Shearing of Las Vegas, who was elected in 1995. Shearing was also the first woman ever elected to the district court in 1983.

Q: Who were the only candidates elected governor of Nevada with less than a majority of votes cast?

A: There have been four "minority" governors: John Jones (1894), from the Silver Party, who garnered forty-nine and nine-tenths percent; Reinhold Sadler (1898), also from the Silver Party, who received thirty-five and seven-tenths percent of the vote, in a three-way split with Democrats and Republicans; Democrat Emmet D. Boyle (1914), who received forty-four and seven-tenths percent of the vote, with the Republicans and Socialists splitting the rest; and Democrat Mike O'Callaghan (1970), who gathered forty-eight and one-tenth percent of the vote, with the rest split between Republicans and Independents.

Q: What former Las Vegas advertising executive served as the U.S. ambassador to Iceland during President George H. Bush's term?

A: Sig Rogich, a successful Las Vegas advertising man, was a member of President Bush's campaign advertising team and served as ambassador to Iceland from June 1992 to January 1993.

Q: Where did U.S. Senator William Stewart propose to move Nevada's state capital in the 1880s?

A: Senator Stewart, from Nevada, proposed moving the state capital to Winnemucca because he was attempting to annex Idaho to Nevada. He wanted the seat of state government to be more centrally located for the new, larger state of Nevada.

Q: In how many presidential elections has Nevada voted for the candidates who prevailed?

A: In twenty-nine of thirty-six presidential elections since 1864, Nevada has sided with the winning candidates (a success rate of more than eighty percent). In fact, since 1912, Nevada has backed the losing party only once, in 1976, when Nevadans favored Republicans Gerald Ford and Robert Dole over winners Jimmy Carter and Walter Mondale.

Q: What was the name of the controversial missile system to be built under 25,000 square miles of western Utah and central Nevada?

A: Proposed by President Jimmy Carter in 1979, the "MX" missile system was to include two hundred intercontinental ballistic missile launch sites at various underground locations throughout the two states. Missiles were to be shifted from site to site to foil detection by the Soviet Union. The proposal fueled concerns about its tremendous costs and impact on the desert ecology, including Nevada's limited water resources. The plan was withdrawn by President Ronald Reagan in 1981.

Q: What was the Sagebrush Rebellion?

A: The Sagebrush Rebellion was a movement, started in 1979, to reclaim federal land in the western U.S. The grass-roots effort was sparked when Congress passed the Federal Land Policy and Management Act in 1976, which changed the status of public lands from land held in trust by the federal government pending disposal, to land permanently controlled by the U.S. Department of Interior. In 1979, the Nevada legislature approved a bill declaring all public lands in Nevada were property of the state. Not surprisingly, the claim was rejected by the federal government.

Q: What Nevada U.S. Senator founded the city of Santa Monica, California?

A: Santa Monica was founded by Senator John P. Jones, who was Nevada's Senator for thirty years (1873 to 1903), despite the fact he only nominally resided in the state. Jones was former superintendent and part owner of Virginia City's Crown Point Mine.

Q: What was the shortest legislative session in Nevada history?

A: On September 13, 1980, the Nevada state legislature met for just over four hours to consider an amendment to the bi-state Tahoe Regional Planning Compact.

Photo of Rex Bell [left] standing with future President Richard Nixon, who is shaking hands with Governor Grant Sawyer.

Photo courtesy Nevada Historical Society

Q: What former cowboy movie star was elected Nevada's lieutenant governor in 1954?

A: Rex Bell, former cowboy film star, who owned a large southern Nevada ranch, was elected lieutenant governor in 1954, and reelected in 1958. He died in 1962, while campaigning for governor.

Q: What was the only year that Nevada held an annual legislative session?

A: In 1960, the Nevada state legislature held its only annual session (not including special sessions, which must be called by the governor). Two years before, voters had approved a constitutional amendment providing for annual sessions of the legislature, but the law was reversed by voter initiative in 1960, following the only annual session ever held.

Q: What U.S. Senator from Nevada was rumored to have died before his reelection?

A: Senator Key Pittman, who actually died five days after his reelection in 1940, is the subject of a frequently repeated myth that he died before the election and his friends kept his body in an ice-filled bathtub in a room at Reno's Riverside Hotel until after the election. The truth was that just prior to the election Pittman suffered a massive heart attack, which was hidden from the public. Doctors knew he was dying but chose to keep silent.

Q: In what year did the Nevada state assembly have an equal number of members who were Democrats and Republicans, requiring it to elect co-speakers?

A: In 1995, the assembly had twenty-one Democrats and twenty-one Republicans, the only time in the state's history that the lower house had the same number of members from each party. As a result, it selected co-speakers as well as co-chairpersons for every committee.

Q: Who was the longest-serving, elected statewide constitutional officeholder?

A: Democrat Robert "Bob" J. Miller served ten years from 1989 to 1999, longer than any other governor. Elected Lieutenant Governor in 1987, Miller became Acting Governor on January 3, 1989, when former Governor Richard Bryan was elected to the U.S. Senate. He was re-elected twice in 1991 and 1995.

George Wingfield

Photo courtesy of Nevada Historical Society

Q: Who was once called the "Napoleon of Nevada Finance," the "Sagebrush Caesar," and "King George" because of his enormous financial and political power during the early part of the twentieth century?

A: George Wingfield who once owned most of Goldfield's mines, nearly all of the state's banks as well as hotels and other businesses, was described in those terms in various newspaper and magazine articles in the 1920s and 1930s. His empire collapsed during the Great Depression when his banks failed and in 1935 he filed for bankruptcy. Within five years, however, he had satisfied his creditors and amassed a second fortune from mining ventures. He maintained a low profile in his later years and died at the age of 83 in 1959.

Q: Who was the youngest person ever to be elected Nevada's governor?

A: Emmet Boyle, who served as governor from 1915 to 1922, was thirty-five years old when elected to the office.

Governor Emmet Boyle

Photo courtesy of Nevada Historical Society

Q: Who was the longest serving governor in Nevada history?

A: Democrat Robert J. "Bob" Miller, has served ten years from 1989 to 1999, more than nine, longer than any other governor. Elected Lieutenant Governor in 1987, Miller became acting governor on January 3, 1989, when former Governor Richard Bryan, was elected to the U.S. Senate. He was re-elected twice, in 1991 and 1995.

Q: What unique ballot category has existed on Nevada's ballots since 1976?

A: Since that year, it has been possible to register displeasure with all candidates for an office by voting "none of the above."

Q: Who was the oldest person ever to be elected Nevada's governor?

A: Lewis Rice Bradley, who served as governor from 1871 to 1878, was sixty-six years old when elected to the office.

Q: Following what census did Nevada finally qualify for a second seat in the U.S. House of Representatives?

A: Nevada finally got its second congressional seat after the 1980 census.

Q: What Nevada lieutenant governor was elected in 1982 as a Democrat but became a Republican shortly after his victory?

A: Reno businessman Robert Cashell, formerly a member of the University of Nevada Board of Regents, was elected lieutenant governor as a Democrat but switched parties within a year after his election. He did not seek reelection.

Q: What Nevada governor was elected by the largest percentage margin of victory?

A: Governor Mike O'Callaghan was reelected to a second term in 1974 with an amazing sixty-seven and four-tenths percent of the vote in the general election. He defeated Republican Shirley Crumpler and Independent J. R. Houston.

**Anne Martin, front seat passenger, in Nevada during
a run for U.S. Senate in 1920.**

Photo courtesy of Nevada Historical Society

Q: What Nevada suffrage leader became the first woman to run
for the U.S. Senate in Nevada?

A: Anne Martin, who in 1914, had been instrumental in passage
of a ballot measure granting women the right to vote, twice ran
for the Senate as an Independent candidate. In a special
election to fill the unexpired term of the late Senator Francis G.
Newlands, she garnered 4,603 votes out of 25,563 cast, to lose
to Democrat Charles B. Henderson in 1918. Two years later
she ran against Senator Henderson once again, picking up
4,981 votes. This time, however, Henderson lost to former
Governor Tasker Oddie (Republican) by 1,148 votes. Martin's
presence in the race is considered to have been one of the
factors in Henderson's defeat.

Q: Who holds the record for serving the most times in the Nevada state assembly?

A: Former Assemblyman Joe Dini of Yerington holds the record for serving the most terms. Dini was first elected in 1966 and, was re-elected to eighteen consecutive two-year terms. He also holds the record for longest-serving Speaker of the Assembly, having been elected to that post eight times.

Q: Who holds the record for being the longest serving member of the Nevada state senate?

A: The longest serving member of the state senate was William F. Dressler of Douglas County, who served for twenty-eight years from 1919 to 1946.

Q: Who holds the all-time record in Nevada for combined legislative service (assembly and senate)?

A: Senator Lawrence E. Jacobsen of Gardnerville, who, between 1963 and 2003, served in the assembly for sixteen years and in the senate for twenty-four years, for a total of 40 years in the Nevada state legislature.longest.

Q: Who is the only First Lady born in Nevada?

A: Patricia Nixon, wife of President Richard Nixon, was born Thelma Catherine (Patricia was a nickname she later adopted) Ryan on March 16, 1912, in a small mining camp near Ely.

Q: Who was the first Nevada U.S. Senator in sixty years (since the beginning of the direct election of senators) to retire voluntarily from his position?

A: In 1974, Senator Alan Bible (Democrat) retired after twenty years in the Senate. All others had either died in office or been defeated. In 1954, he won a special election to fill the unexpired term of Senator Patrick McCarran (Democrat), who died earlier that year. He was reelected three times (1956, 1962 and 1968).

Q: What Baseball Hall-of-Famer was married to the daughter of Nevada's lone Congressman in 1914?

A: Walter "Big Train" Johnson was the ballplayer. Johnson, who pitched for the Washington Senators from 1907 to 1927 and was elected to the National Baseball Hall of Fame in 1936, married Hazel Lee Roberts, daughter of Congressman Edwin Ewing Roberts of Reno, on June 24, 1914.

FASCINATING FACTS
Vital Statistics of the Sagebrush State

❖❖❖❖❖❖❖❖❖❖❖❖❖❖❖❖❖❖❖❖❖❖

Q: About how many marriages are performed each year in Las Vegas?

A: About 119,000 annually, with Valentine's Day being the busiest wedding day of the year.

Q: How large is Nevada?

A: Nevada is 110,540 square miles or 70,264,320 acres. It measures 485 miles from top to bottom and is 315 miles across at its widest point.

Q: What city has the highest rate of water consumption in the world?

A: Las Vegas uses a staggering 375 gallons of water per person per day. This is twice as high as Phoenix and four times the rate of Philadelphia.

Q: How many people live in Nevada?

A: According to the Nevada State Demographer, in 2003, 2,296,566 people were living in the Silver State.

Q: What is Nevada's most populated county?

A: Clark County, the southern Nevada county that includes Las Vegas, is home to nearly sixty-nine percent of the state's population, or 1,620,748 inhabitants (2003 Nevada State Demographer).

Q: Name the least populated county.

A: Esmeralda County, with 1,116 residents in 2003. Tucked away in the southwestern edge of the state, Esmeralda County has less than one-tenth of the one-percent of the state's population.

Q: What is the average temperature in Las Vegas?

A: The average is 66.3º F.

Q: What is the average annual rainfall in Las Vegas?

A: The average is 4.13 inches of rain.

Q: What is the elevation of Las Vegas?

A: Las Vegas is 2,000 feet. Reno, by comparison, is 4,498 feet.

Q: About how many people move into Clark County each month?

A: In 2003, roughly 6,000 people moved into the county each month.

Q: After whom was Clark County (Las Vegas) named?

A: William A. Clark, U.S. Senator from Montana in the early twentieth century. Clark built the San Pedro, Los Angeles and Salt Lake Railroad, which helped to establish the city of Las Vegas in 1905.

Q: Where does Las Vegas rank in size compared to other U.S. cities?

A: In 2003, Las Vegas ranked 30th largest, just ahead of Tucson, Arizona.

Q: True or False? Las Vegas was the fastest growing city in the U.S. between 1990 and 2000?

A: True. Las Vegas grew 85.2 percent during the decade of the 1990s, from 258,295 to 478,434 in population.

Nevada gold mining operation

Q: Where does Nevada rank in silver production?

A: Since gold and silver are frequently found together, it's no surprise that Nevada ranks first in silver production in the U.S. In 2003, the state produced 10.2 million troy ounces of silver.

Q: Where does Nevada rank in terms of barite production?

A: First in the nation, with 480,000 tons mined in 2000. Barite is used to produce barium as well as in making paint.

Q: Where does Nevada rank in gold production?

A: In 2003, the state ranked first in gold production, producing 7.32 million troy ounces, which was about sixty-six percent of all the gold mined in the U.S. If Nevada were a country, it would rank third, behind South Africa and Australia, as a gold-producing region.

Q: What is the official state animal?

A: The official animal is the desert bighorn sheep (*Ovis canadensis nelsoni*), which populates many of the state's highest mountain ranges.

Q: What is Nevada's official state bird?

A: The beautiful mountain bluebird (*Sialia Currucoides*) is the state bird.

Q: What is Nevada's official state fish?

A: This special fish is the Lahontan cutthroat trout (*Salmo clarki henshawi*).

Q: What is the official state grass?

A: The official grass is Indian ricegrass (*Oryzopsis hymenoides*), once an important part of the diet of the state's native peoples.

Bighorn Sheep
Photo by Las Vegas News Bureau

Q: What are Nevada's two official state trees?

A: The piñon pine (*Pinus monophylla*) and bristlecone pine (*Pinus aristata*) are the state trees. Bristlecone pines can live to be more than 4,000 years old.

Q: What is the official state reptile?

A: The desert tortoise (*Gopherus agassizi*) is the official reptile. The tortoise is an endangered species found in the southern part of the state and can live to be more than seventy years old.

Q: What is Nevada's official state flower?

A: Sagebrush (*Artemisia tridentata*), a member of the aster plant family, is the state flower.

Q: What is Nevada's official state fossil?

A: Nevada is the only state to possess a complete, fifty-five-foot-long skeleton of this extinct prehistoric reptile, Ichthyosaur. Fossils are displayed at the Berlin-Ichthyosaur State Park in central Nevada.

Q: What is the official state artifact?

A: The Lovelock Cave Tule Duck Decoy was designated the official state artifact in 1995.

Q: What is the official state metal?

A: The vast deposits of silver found near Virginia City sparked a major mining boom in the 1850s, which provided the impetus for the settlement of Nevada.

Q: What is the official state precious stone?

A: The Virgin Valley black fire opal, found only in northern Nevada, was designated the state precious gem in 1987.

Q: What is Nevada's official state rock?

A: The official state rock, sandstone, is found throughout Nevada.

Big Sagebrush
Photo by Nevada State Highway Department

Ichthyosaur Fossil
Photo by Ken Evans

Q: What is the official state semi-precious stone?

A: Turquoise, often called the "Jewel of the Desert" and found in many places in the state, is Nevada's official semi-precious stone.

Q: What is the median price of an existing single-family home in Las Vegas?

A: $250,000 in 2004. In Reno, it was $278,750.

Q: How many licensed doctors operate in Nevada?

A: In 2001, there were more than 4,000 licensed doctors in the state (or about one doctor for every 600 residents).

Q: What percentage of Nevada is controlled by the federal government?

A: The United States government controls 82.3 percent of Nevada, or nearly 60 million acres.

Q: How many people lived in Las Vegas in 1910?

A: 945.

Q: True or False–Las Vegas has the most churches per capita of any major American city?

A: False. While civic leaders promoted this alleged fact for many decades to counter the city's sinful reputation, a 1997 *Las Vegas Review-Journal* article found that the city had 586 churches, which yielded a ratio of one church per 1,910 residents. By comparison, Memphis, TN, had a ratio of one church for every 875 residents, and there are likely other cities with more churches per capita.

Q: How many conventions are held in Las Vegas each year?

A: About 24,000 annually, according to the Las Vegas Convention and Visitors Authority.

Q: What is Nevada's average monthly hotel and motel occupancy rate?

A: The statewide monthly average rate is about eighty percent, according to the Nevada Commission on Tourism.

Q: Every year, about how many vehicles enter Nevada by way of Interstates, U.S. and State highways?

A: About 25 million.

Q: What is the average nightly room rate in Las Vegas

A: In 2003, it was about $83.00.

Q: In 2003, about how many passengers arrived and departed from Nevada's airports?

A: About 41 million, according to the Nevada Commission on Tourism.

Q: How many miles of paved streets and highways can be found in Nevada?

A: At last count, there were 49,702 miles of paved roads in the state.

Q: Where is Nevada located in terms of longitude and latitude?

A: Nevada is located in the zone from 114 to 120 degrees longitude (West of Greenwich) and between 35 and 42 degrees north latitude.

Q: Despite the fact Nevada has been the fastest growing state during the past decade, what is the population density of the state?

A: In 2003, there were 20.77 people per square mile in Nevada.

Q: Of all the states, Nevada has the lowest percentage of native born residents. What is the ratio?

A: Only one of every five Nevada residents was born in the state. This compares with the national average of one in three Americans living in their native state.

Q: How many daily newspapers are published in Nevada?

A: There are nine daily newspapers in the state including: *Nevada Appeal, Elko Daily Free Press, Lahontan Valley News & Fallon Eagle Standard, Las Vegas Review-Journal, Las Vegas Sun, Nevada Daily Legal News, Reno Gazette-Journal, Sparks Tribune* and *Humboldt Sun.*

Q: What percentage of Nevada's population resides in Las Vegas, Reno and Carson City?

A: Eighty percent of the state's population is concentrated in these areas.

Q: What is the most harvested crop in Nevada?

A: In 1997, 1,458,687 tons of dry alfalfa hay was harvested in the state.

Q: True of False: Nevada has an official state soil?

A: True: In 2001, the Nevada State Legislature designated the Orovada Series Soil as the official state soil. It is described as coarse-loamy, mixed, superactive, mesic Durinodic Xeric Haplocambids. It is found in northern and central Nevada. Orovada soil grows most of the crops in the state and is considered prime farming land because it contains volcanic ash that reduces the amount of water needed for irrigation.

Q: Where does Nevada rank nationally in terms of revenue generated by agriculture?

A: Nevada ranked forty-seventh in 2000.

Q: What Nevada attraction ranks thirty-fourth in the U.S. in amusement/theme park attendance?

A: The Adventuredome at Circus Circus in Las Vegas, which had 2,977,000 visitors in 2001.

Q: True or False: Nevada has an official state Tartan?

A: True: In 2001, the Nevada State Legislature designated a tartan pattern designed by Richard Zygmunt Pawlowski as the official state tartan. The colors and design represent the various state symbols.

The Adventuredome at Circus Circus in Las Vegas is one of Nevada's most popular attractions.

Photo courtesy of the Las Vegas News Bureau.

Q: How many legal holidays does Nevada observe?

A: New Year's Day, Martin Luther King Jr. Holiday, Presidents' Day, Memorial Day, Independence Day, Labor Day, Nevada Day, Veteran's Day, Thanksgiving and Christmas.

Q: How many official state flag designs has Nevada had?

A: Four. The first, used from 1905 to 1915, incorporated a simple design with gold and silver stars and the words "Nevada," "Silver" and "Gold" on a blue background. The second, in use from 1915 to 1929, retained a blue back-ground but featured an elaborate version of the state seal in the center. The third, used from 1929 to 1991, had a cobalt blue background with a simple design of two sprigs of sagebrush, a silver star, a banner with the words "Battle Born" and the state's name encircling the star. The fourth and current flag is a slight revision of this design, with the state's name beneath the star.

Q: What are Nevada's nicknames?

A: Nevada is known as the "Sagebrush State" and the "Silver State."

Q: What are Nevada's official state colors?

A: Silver and blue represent the importance of the mineral, silver, to the state's development and the wide open blue skies.

Q: What city was named the best small town in America in a 1992 book called *The 100 Best Small Towns in America*?

A: The northeastern Nevada town of Elko was honored with that designation by the book's author, Norman Crampton.

Q: How many cattle are estimated to be roving Nevada's range land?

A: There are about 520,000 cattle in the state.

Q: How many calves are generally born each year in Nevada?

A: Approximately 220,000 calves are born each year.

Branding time at a typical Nevada cattle operation

Q: How many cattle ranches are located in Nevada?
A: There are 1,600 cattle ranches.

Q: About how many sheep and lambs are there in Nevada?
A: There are about 96,000 sheep and lambs in the state.

Q: How many hogs and pigs are estimated to be in Nevada?
A: There are about 7,400 hogs and pigs in the state.

Q: Approximately how many turkeys are raised and sold in Nevada each year?
A: About 670 every year.

Q: How does Nevada rank in size, compared with other states?
A: Nevada is the seventh largest state, with 110,540 square miles.

Q: By what percentage did Nevada's population grow from 1990 to 2000?
A: The state grew at 66.3 percent (first in the nation), from a population of 1,201,833 to 1,998,257.

Q: About how many babies are born in Nevada each year?
A: In 2002, 32,571 babies were born in the state. There are also about 15,000 deaths each year.

Q: What is the graduation rate of Nevada's public high schools?
A: About seventy-four percent. Nevada ranks twenty-first in the U.S. in graduating its high school students.

Q: How much money does the state of Nevada receive back from every dollar sent to the federal government by Nevada taxpayers?
A: Nevada receives $.69 for every dollar sent to Washington. In fact, Nevada ranks forty-ninth among all states in this regard.

Q: How much revenue does the state of Nevada receive in state income taxes?
A: None. Nevada has no state income tax.

Q: How many housing units can be found in Nevada?
A: In 2002, Nevada had 901,597 houses, condos and other types of housing units. 2.62 persons lived in each household.

Q: How many area codes are in Nevada?
A: Two, 702 (southern Nevada) and 775 (northern and much of rural Nevada).

Q: What is the per capita personal income in Nevada?

A: It is $30,529, according to the 2000 U.S. Census.

Q: What percentage of Nevadans live below the federal poverty level?

A: In 1999, 10.5 percent of Nevadans lived below the poverty level.

Q: Where does Nevada rank among the states in terms of how many people it sends to prison?

A: Nevada ranks eighth in the nation, with an incarceration rate of 18 prisoners per 100,000 residents.

Q: True or False - Since 1976, Nevada has executed as many criminals as the states of New Jersey, Connecticut, Wyoming, New Mexico, Colorado, Idaho, Tennessee, Montana, New York, South Dakota, New Hampshire, Oregon and Kentucky combined?

A: True: Since 1976, Nevada has executed 11 criminals while New Jersey, Connecticut, New York, South Dakota, and New Hampshire have executed none, Wyoming, New Mexico, Colorado, Idaho, and Tennessee have each executed one, and Montana, Oregon, and Kentucky have each executed two.

Q: Does Nevada have more male or female residents?

A: According to the 2000 U.S. Census, Nevada has more males. The state had 1,018,051 men (50.9 percent) and 980,206 women (49.1 percent). Of all the states, Nevada has the second highest ratio of males to females, 103.9 per 100, behind Alaska, which has a ratio of 107 to 100.

Q: Name four state capitals that have the word "city" in their names?

A: Carson City, Nevada, Oklahoma City, Oklahoma, Salt Lake City, Utah, Jefferson City, Missouri.

Q: True or False - Nevada has the highest suicide rate in the nation?

A: False. According to the Centers for Disease Control, in 2003 Nevada ranked second in the nation, behind Alaska, with just over twenty-one suicides per 100,000 residents. Historically, Nevada and Alaska have been either first or second in suicide rates for most of the last decade.

Q: What is the rate of homeownership in Nevada?

A: According to the 2000 U.S. Census, 60.9 percent of Nevadans own their own homes.

Q: In what year did Las Vegas officially surpass Reno in population?

A: Las Vegas was officially recognized as the larger city in the 1960 U.S. Census. Las Vegas reached a population of 64,405, compared to Reno's 51,470.

Q: How many Nevadans are older than 65?

A: In 2000, eleven percent were senior citizens, while 25.6 percent were under 18 years old.

Q: Where in the world was the supersonic land-speed record set?

A: The Black Rock Desert, north of Gerlach, was the site of the first breaking of the sound barrier by a vehicle on land. The run was made on October 13, 1997 in the rocket-powered Thrust SSC car, driven by Andrew Green of England. Two days later, Green duplicated the feat and set the official world land-speed record with two runs averaging 763.035 miles per hour.

Q: What percentage of Nevadans were born outside of the United States?

A: According to the 2000 U.S. Census, 15.8 percent of Nevadans were foreign-born.

Q: True or False - In 2002, Nevada ranked last in the nation in high school graduation rate?

A: False: Nevada actually ranks 39th nationally in high school graduation rate, with 62 percent, according to the National Center for Public Policy and Higher Education. The national average is 68 percent. In the same study, however, Nevada did rank last in the number of students who went directly to college after high school graduation.

Q: How many boats are registered in Nevada?

A: Even though Nevada is the driest state in the nation, there were 61,123 boats licensed in the state in 2001.

Q: What is the largest library in the state?

A: The University of Nevada Library, which serves both the University of Nevada, Reno and the University of Nevada, Las Vegas, is the largest book repository, with more than 800,000 volumes.

Q: What is Nevada's largest bank?

A: The Nevada division of Wells Fargo Bank.

Q: When did the first automobile cross the Sierra Nevada?

A: On May 27, 1901, a 12-horsepower Winton touring car, driven by automaker Alexander Winton and newspaperman Charles R. Shanks, traveled from San Francisco to Reno.

Q: When was the first road race staged in Nevada?

A: On August 31, 1913, Earl Jackson and Chester Milberry, both of Reno, won the first organized road race, which was a seventy-mile loop from Carson City to Reno, then to Virginia City and back to Carson City. It took the winners three hours and twenty-two minutes to complete the drive.

Q: How many vehicles are registered in Nevada?

A: In 2000, there were 1,652,969 passenger vehicles registered in the state—or nearly one for every person. Additionally, there were 1,385,696 licensed drivers in the state.

Q: What is the official state song and who wrote it?

A: "Home Means Nevada," written by Mrs. Bertha Raffetto of Reno, was named the state song in 1933.

Q: What is Nevada's official motto?

A: "All for Our Country," which appears in the state seal, is the official motto.

Q: How many stars can be found on the Nevada State Seal?

A: The seal's thirty-six stars symbolize that Nevada was the thirty-sixth state.

Nevada State Seal

QUICK FACTS ABOUT NEVADA

❖❖❖❖❖❖❖❖❖❖❖❖❖❖❖❖❖❖❖❖❖❖❖

STATE NICKNAME: Silver State and Sagebrush State

STATE MOTTO: "All for our country"

STATE SONG: *Home Means Nevada*

STATE COLORS: Blue and Silver

STATE FLOWER: Sagebrush Bloom

STATE TREE: Bristlecone Pine or Single Leaf Piñon

STATE GRASS: Indian Ricegrass

STATE BIRD: Mountain Bluebird

STATE MAMMAL: Desert Bighorn

STATE REPTILE: Desert Tortoise

STATE GEMS: Turquoise and Black Fire Opal

STATE MINERAL: Silver

STATE ROCK: Sandstone

OFFICIAL FISH: Lahontan Cutthroat

OFFICIAL FOSSIL: Ichthyosaur

ELEVATION: The highest point is Boundary Peak at a height of 13,143 feet. The lowest point is the Colorado River at the Nevada-California-Arizona border at an elevation of 470 feet.

SIZE: 109,590 square miles. Seventh largest state measuring 320 miles wide by about 483 miles long.

STATE ADMITTANCE TO UNION: Nevada is the 36th state and was admitted on October 31, 1864

BIBLIOGRAPHY

◆◆◆◆◆◆◆◆◆◆◆◆◆◆◆◆◆◆◆◆◆◆
◆◆◆◆◆◆◆◆◆◆◆◆◆◆◆◆◆◆◆◆◆◆

Basso, Dave. *Nevada Historical Marker Guidebook*. Sparks, Nevada: Falcon Hill Press, 1986.

Bowers, Michael W. *The Sagebrush State*. Reno, Nevada: University of Nevada Press, 1996.

Canfield, Gae Whitney. *Sarah Winnemucca of the Northern Paiutes*. Norman, Oklahoma: University of Oklahoma Press, 1983.

Carleson, Helen. *Nevada Place Names*. Reno, Nevada: University of Nevada Press, 1974.

Castleman, Deke. *Nevada Handbook*. Sixth Edition. Emeryville, California: Avalon Travel, 2001.

_____. *Las Vegas*. Oakland, California: Compass America Guides, Inc., 1991.

Cerveri, Doris. *With Curry's Compliments, The Story of Abraham Curry*. Elko, Nevada: Nostalgia Press, 1990.

Cohen, Shayne Del. *Nevada Tribal History and Government*. Reno. Nevada: Western Printing and Publishing Co., 1981.

Coyner, Alan and Doug Driesner. *Major Mines of Nevada*. Nevada Division of Minerals, 2000.

Elliott, Russell. *History of Nevada*. Revised. Lincoln, Nebraska: University of Nebraska Press, 1987.

Hall, Shawn. *A Guide to the Ghost Towns and Mining Camps of Nye County*. New York, New York: Dodd, Mead & Company, 1981.

_____. *Romancing Nevada's Past: Ghost Towns and Historic Sites of Eureka, Lander and White Pine Counties*. Reno, Nevada: University of Nevada Press, 1994.

_____. *Old Heart of Nevada: Ghost Towns and Mining Camps of Elko County*, Reno, Nevada: University of Nevada Press, 1998.

_____.*Preserving the Glory Days: Ghost Towns and Mining Camps of Nye County, Nevada*, Reno, Nevada: University of Nevada Press, 1999.

Heller, Dean. *Political History of Nevada*, Nevada: Nevada Secretary of State, 1996.

Hess, Alan. *Viva Las Vegas*. San Francisco, California: Chronicle Books, 1993.

History of the Nevada State Capital and Governor's Mansion. Carson City, Nevada: State of Nevada, 1988.

Hittman, Michael. *Wovoka and the Ghost Dance*. Carson City, Nevada: Grace Dangberg Foundation Inc. 1990.

Howard, Anne Bail. *The Long Campaign*. Reno, Nevada: University of Nevada Press, 1985.

Johnson, Edward C. *Walker River Paiutes, A Tribal History*. Schurz, Nevada: Walker River Paiute Tribe, 1978.

Knepp, Donn. *Las Vegas, The Entertainment Capital*. Menlo Park, California: Lane Publishing Co., 1987.

Kling, Dwayne. *The Rise of the Biggest Little City: An Encyclopedic History of Reno Gambling, 1931-1981*. Reno, Nevada: University of Nevada Press, 2000.

Land, Barbara and Myrick. *Short History of Reno*. Reno, Nevada: University of Nevada Press, 1995.

_____.*Short History of Las Vegas*. Reno, Nevada: University of Nevada Press, 1999.

Lanner, Ronald M. *Trees of the Great Basin, A Natural History*. Reno, Nevada: University of Nevada Press, 1984.

Lewis, Oscar. *The Town That Died Laughing*. Boston, Massachusetts: Little, Brown and Co., 1955.

Lingenfelter, Richard E. and Gash, Karen Rix. *The Newspapers of Nevada*. Reno, Nevada: University of Nevada Press, 1984.

Lord, Eliot. *Comstock Mining and Miners*. Berkeley, California: Howell-North, Reprint of 1883 edition, 1959.

Lynch, Don and Thompson, David. *Battle Born Nevada*. Carson City, Nevada: Grace Dangberg Foundation Inc., 1994.

McCracken, Robert D. *Las Vegas The Great American Playground*. Reno, Nevada: University of Nevada Press, 1997.

McDonald, Douglas. *Virginia City and the Silver Region of the Comstock Lode*. Las Vegas, Nevada: Nevada Publications, 1982.

_____. *Short History of Las Vegas*. Reno, Nevada: University of Nevada Press, 1999.

McLane, Alvin R. *Silent Cordilleras*. Reno, Nevada: Camp Nevada, 1978.

Merriman, Marion and Lerude, Warren. *American Commander in Spain*. Reno, Nevada: University of Nevada Press, 1986.

Moreno, Richard. *The Backyard Traveler, 54 Outings in Northern Nevada*. Carson City, Nevada: Carson City Children's Museum, 1991.

_____. *Roadside History of Nevada*. Missoula, Montana: Mountain Press, 2000.

_____. *The Backyard Traveler Returns, 62 Outings in Southern, Eastern and Historic Nevada*. Carson City, Nevada: Carson City Children's Museum, 1992.

Mozingo, Hugh N. *Shrubs of the Great Basin, A Natural History*. Reno, Nevada: University of Nevada Press, 1987.

Murbarger, Nell. *Ghosts of the Glory Trail*. Las Vegas, Nevada: Nevada Publications, 1983.

Myrick, David F. *Railroads of Nevada and Eastern California, Volume I*. Reno, Nevada: University of Nevada Press, 1992.

_____. *Railroads of Nevada and Eastern California, Volume II*. Reno, Nevada: University of Nevada Press, 1992.

Nevada Commission of Tourism. *Discover the Facts*. 2003-04.

Nevada Department of Agriculture, *1997 Census of Agriculture*.

Nevada Gaming Control Board and Nevada Gaming Commission, *2001 Information Sheet*.

Nevada Historical Society Quarterly

Nevada Magazine

Nevada Statistical Abstract. Carson City, Nevada: Nevada Department of Administration, 1992.

Newe: A Western Shoshone History. Reno, Nevada: Inter-Tribal Council of Nevada, 1976.

Numa: A Northern Paiute History. Reno, Nevada: Inter-Tribal Council of Nevada, 1976.

_____. *Old Heart of Nevada: Ghost Towns and Mining Camps of Elko County*. Reno, Nevada: University of Nevada Press, 1998.

Paher, Stanley. *Las Vegas, As It Began—As It Grew*. Las Vegas, Nevada: Nevada Publications, 1971.

Paher, Stanley. *Nevada Ghost Towns and Mining Camps*. Las Vegas, Nevada: Nevada Publications, 1984.

_____. *Preserving the Glory Days: Ghost Towns and Mining Camps of Nye County*. Reno, Nevada: University of Nevada Press, 1999.

Raymond, C. Elizabeth. George Wingfield, *Owner and Operator of Nevada*. Reno, Nevada: University of Nevada Press, 1992.

Rocha, Guy Louis. Nevada State Archives, *Historical Myth of the Month Columns*, http://dmla.clan.nv.us/docs/nsla/archives/myth/.

Rowley, William D. Reno: *Hub of the Washoe Country*. Northridge, California: Windsor Publications, 1984.

Ryser, Fred A. *Birds of the Great Basin*. Reno, Nevada: University of Nevada Press, 1985.

Shamberger, Hugh. *Goldfield*. Carson City, Nevada: Nevada Historical Press, 1982.

Shepperson, Wilbur S. *Mirage-Land*. Reno, Nevada: University of Nevada Press, 1992.

Sigler, William F. and Sigler, John W. *Fishes of the Great Basin*. Reno, Nevada: University of Nevada Press, 1987.

State of Nevada Transportation Facts and Figures, January 2001.

Swackhamer, William D. *Political History of Nevada*. Carson City, Nevada: Secretary of State's Office, 1986.

Thompson, David. *Nevada Events 1776–1985*. Carson City, Nevada: Grace Dangberg Foundation Inc., 1987.

Thompson and West's 1881 History of Nevada. Reproduction. San Diego, California: Howell-North, 1958.

Toll, David. *The Compleat Nevada Traveler.* Gold Hill, Nevada: Gold Hill Publishing Co., 1993.

Twain, Mark. *Roughing It.* New York, New York: New American Library, 1962.

Wheeler, Sessions S. *The Desert Lake.* Caldwell, Idaho: The Caxton Printers, 1987.

_____. *The Nevada Desert.* Caldwell, Idaho: The Caxton Printers, 1982.

World Almanac and Book of Facts 2002. New York, New York: World Almanac Books, 2002.

WPA Guide to Nevada. Portland, Oregon: Binford and Mort Publishers, 1940.

Wuerthner, George. *Nevada Mountain Ranges.* Helena, Montana: American & World Geographic Publishing, 1992.

Zanjani, Sally. *A Mine of Her Own: Women Prospectors in the American West, 1850-1950.* Lincoln, Nebraska: University of Nebraska Press, 1997.

ADDITIONAL REFERENCES & RESOURCES

❖❖❖❖❖❖❖❖❖❖❖❖❖❖❖❖❖❖❖❖❖❖❖❖

2000 United States Census.

City of Las Vegas.

City of Reno.

Las Vegas Review-Journal.

Las Vegas Sun.

Nevada Division of Minerals

Nevada Magazine

Nevada Office of Historic Preservation

Nevada Secretary of State's Office

Reno Gazette-Journal

Rocha, Guy Louis, Nevada State Archives, *Historical Myth of the Month* Columns, http://dmla.clan.nv.us/docs/nsla/archives/myth.

State of Nevada Demographer

USA Today

www.burningman.com

www.leg.state.nv.us

INDEX

A

A Cup of Tea in Pamplona – 40
Abraham Lincoln Brigade – 39
Adams House – 135
Adams V, John Quincy – 135
Adams, John Quincy – 135
Adams, Quincy – 135
Adams, Rufus – 135
Adaven, Nevada – 110
Adventuredome – 195
advertising campaigns – 52
aerial acrobatics – 117
African-American settlers – 17
Agassi, Andre – 71
agriculture – 24,26,30,142,160,194
air flights – 37
air Races – 109
airmail service – 37
alcohol – 106
Alexander, Ben – 72
alfalfa – 24
alfalfa hay – 194
alkali flats – 153
"All for Our Country" – 202, 204
All Quiet on the Western Front – 72
Alta Toquima – 106
Altube, Pedro – 41
ambassador to Iceland – 176
American City, Nevada – 92
American Flat – 92,93,166

American Society of Civil Engineers – 26
amphibians – 154
amusement/theme parks – 195
An Innocent Man – 66
Anaho Island – 148,164
Anasazi – 125,132
Ancient Ones – 125
Andrews Sisters – 49
Angel Lake – 153
annexation – 99,176
annual precipitation – 148
antelope – 146
The Apache – 52
Arabian horses – 144
Arc Dome – 106
arches – 104
architects – 36,66,112,114
Area 51 – 105
area codes – 198
Arizona – 8,12,99,100,114,187
Arizona Territory – 7,8
Army – 21, 128
artifacts – 125,134
artists – 39,137,141
Ash Meadows Amargosa pupfish – 159
Ash Meadows National Wildlife
   Refuge – 159,163
Ash Meadows speckled dace – 159
Ash Springs – 163
Atlanta Braves – 73
Atlantic Ocean – 99

M

ABOUT THE AUTHOR

❖❖❖❖❖❖❖❖❖❖❖❖❖❖❖❖❖❖❖❖❖

Richard Moreno is publisher of *Nevada* magazine and author of *The Backyard Traveler, 54 Outings in Northern Nevada* and *The Backyard Traveler Returns, 62 Outings in Southern, Eastern and Historic Nevada.*

He has lived in Nevada for twelve years. Before joining Nevada magazine in 1992, he worked for more than seven years as director of advertising and public relations and as public information officer for the Nevada Commission on Tourism. In 1987 he won a Travel Industry Association of America public relations award for his "Highway 50 - the Loneliest Road in America" promotion, which put that remote stretch of Nevada road on the map.

Previously, he worked for nearly five years as a newspaper reporter, including three and one-half years at the *Reno Gazette-Journal.* He is former Nevada Press Association "Outstanding Young Journalist of the Year."

Mr. Moreno has a masters degree in journalism from Columbia University and is a member of the Carson City Library Board of Trustees and the Carson City Children's Museum Executive Board.

NOTES

NOTES